# Extensive Reading Handbook

## For Secondary Teachers

Edited with an Introduction by
Gail Ellis and John McRae

PENGUIN ENGLISH

PENGUIN BOOKS

Published by the Penguin Group
Penguin Books Ltd, 27 Wrights Lane, London W8 5TZ, England
Viking Penguin, a division of Penguin Books USA Inc.
375 Hudson Street, New York, New York 10014, USA
Penguin Books Australia Ltd, Ringwood, Victoria, Australia
Penguin Books Canada Ltd, 2801 John Street, Markham, Ontario, Canada L3R 1B4
Penguin Books (NZ) Ltd, 182–190 Wairau Road, Auckland 10, New Zealand

Penguin Books Ltd, Registered Offices: Harmondsworth, Middlesex, England

Published in Penguin Books 1991
10 9 8 7 6 5 4 3 2 1

The publishers would like to thank Jonathan Cape and Unwin Hyman Ltd for
permission to include excerpts from Roald Dahl's *The Twits* and *Charlie and the
Chocolate Factory*, and the Estate of the late Sonia Brownell Orwell and Martin
Secker & Warburg Ltd for 'The Seven Commandments' from George Orwell's
*Animal Farm*.

Printed in England by Clays Ltd, St Ives plc

# Contents

## Part 2 Notes

### Section 1 Primary to Lower Secondary

### Section 2 Lower Secondary

### Section 3 Lower to Upper Secondary

### Editions

*The Twits*, Roald Dahl, Puffin, 1982
*Charlie and the Chocolate Factory*, Roald Dahl, Puffin, 1985
*Animal Farm*, George Orwell, Penguin, 1989
*The Happy Prince and Other Stories*, Oscar Wilde, Puffin, 1962
*Call of the Wild*, Jack London, Puffin, 1982
*Treasure Island*, Robert Louis Stevenson, Puffin, 1987
*Collected Short Stories*, Volume 1, W. Somerset Maugham, Penguin, 1987
*The Red Badge of Courage*, Stephen Crane, Puffin, 1986
*Robinson Crusoe*, Daniel Defoe, Puffin, 1986
*Dracula*, Bram Stoker, Puffin, 1986
*The Adventures of Tom Sawyer*, Mark Twain, Puffin, 1987
*The Adventures of Huckleberry Finn*, Mark Twain, Puffin, 1953

# Part 1  Extensive reading, an introduction

### What is extensive reading?

Extensive reading involves encouraging learners to read a range of materials, read them quickly and well, for pleasure and for language development.

This handbook, with practical notes developed by teachers directly from classroom experience, will help teachers guide students through a range of books from fairly short, fully illustrated fables to more adult full-length novels. How many books any teacher, class or individual student will want to read will depend on many factors. In the first instance enthusiasm on the teacher's part and the conscious development of the *habit* of reading in the student are of paramount importance. Reading leads to reading.

Naturally, constraints of class time, the availability of books and back-up material, and reader motivation often weigh heavily against the development of students' individual reading skills and abilities. But the careful building up of reader familiarity with a variety of books will lead to a wider reading range, encourage individual exploration, and make extensive reading part of a student's education for life.

### Extensive reading and class time

It is in the nature of extensive reading that most of it is done outside class, in the students' own time. But a necessary part of the process of encouraging extensive reading is that initially the reading should be *motivated* and then regularly *monitored*, so that rhythms of reading are built up and class interaction on the reading developed. Reading strategies are also devised, applied and refined during the whole extensive reading process. (*See the section Reading and language acquisition*.)

How much class time can be dedicated to extensive reading must depend on the teaching situation, curriculum requirements and, indeed, on individual teachers and classes. Ideally, half an hour once a week or every ten days should be devoted to extensive reading. This should be interaction and language work, based on what has been read, rather than mere verification that reading has been done, or checking comprehension. Monitoring means following through and leading reading onwards.

### Preparing the learners

Most students need help in making the leap from teacher-guided, close study of short texts to individual reading of whole books. They will probably need preparation in the following three areas:

*Psychological preparation* Activities to encourage thinking about their approaches to reading and building confidence for reading independently.

*Methodological preparation* Training in some of the skills and strategies needed for effective reading.

*Practice in self-direction* Guidance on deciding what to read, how to read, and how to evaluate and monitor progress.

#### Psychological preparation

Many students find reading in a foreign language difficult and laborious. Typical student reactions are: 'There are too many new words I don't understand', 'It takes me too long and I give up', 'I get bored'.

It is important that students are helped to become aware of and to understand, the reasons for these attitudes. Ask them what sort of books they most enjoy reading in their mother tongue and *how* they read them. Then ask about their attempts to read in English and the difficulties they encounter. These questions can also form the basis of an informal discussion, either in English or in the mother tongue. Alternatively, ask students to design a questionnaire to find out about the class's reading habits. Information gathered can enable students to choose appropriate books and identify their reading problems. It can also provide the teacher with useful information on the type of reading strategies you may need to develop in the classroom.

Encourage students to choose books on subjects they are genuinely interested in. Successful reading is affected by the way in which the subject matter relates to a learner's existing cultural and general knowledge or to subject-specific knowledge. The students will be helped in their reading if some of the information is already understood; learning new vocabulary and understanding structure will be aided.

Demonstrate how students can use their background knowledge in reading. For example, the following questions can be asked about *Foxy Fables* to contextualize the story and to relate it to what students already know about fables:

- What is a fable?
- Who are the main characters in a fable?
- Do you know any fables?
- Do you know the names of any people who wrote fables?

Encourage students to think about any book on these lines before they start reading.

Make sure students realize that when reading extensively their objectives should be different to those for studying a short text in class. This will help them form realistic expectations and avoid frustration and disappointment. Allay fears about not understanding every word by emphasizing that 100 per cent comprehension is not necessary to understand the overall meaning. They should use all available clues from the language, the context and from the illustrations – where relevant – to help make sense of the book.

*Methodological preparation*

The skills and strategies required for successful extensive reading can be developed in class time for reading. The following suggestions can help students become aware of strategies such as previewing, predicting, guessing the meaning of unknown words and developing vocabulary.

PREVIEWING

This involves looking at the title and the cover, reading information on the back cover about the story and its author, examining the list of contents or chapter headings, and glancing through the book to get an impression of layout, print size and illustrations. You can show students how to preview by selecting a book and asking questions such as:

- What is the title of the book?
- What do you think it will be about?
- Who is the author?
- Do you know anything about the author?
- Is it an old or a contemporary story? How do you know?
- Do you think you will enjoy the book? Why or why not?
- Do you think you will find it easy or difficult? Why?

Students could also work in groups with different books, using the questions above and then reporting back to the teacher.

PREDICTING

When we read in our mother tongue we predict unconsciously but we do not often transfer this strategy when we read in a foreign language. The title, cover, illustrations and linguistic clues can help us predict vocabulary and the story-line.

*Making use of the title and the cover* Select a book with a clear title and an interesting cover and ask students to predict some of the vocabulary they expect to find. The following words were some suggested by students for *Dracula*: teeth, blood, fangs, horror, frightening. Students may give words in their mother tongue as this would show that they are thinking in the appropriate lexical area. It also provides the teacher with an ideal opportunity to introduce these words, as the need to use them has come from students themselves.

*Making use of illustrations* Students can also be trained to use illustrations to help them understand the text, predict the story-line and acquire new vocabulary. The illustrations in *Foxy Fables* can be used to predict the story-line of each fable. For example, examine the illustrations in 'The Fox and the Stork' and ask students what they think happens in the fable and what they think the moral might be.

*Making use of contextual and linguistic clues* Students can be trained to use context and other signals, such as connectors, sequencers, punctuation and grammar, and their knowledge of the topic, to predict what comes next. Ask students to cover the text and then to uncover one line at a time, guessing the next line before they uncover it. Discuss what helped them to predict the lines.

GUESSING UNKNOWN WORDS
Ask or tell your students which clues they can use to guess the meaning of unknown words. For example, visual support, the position of the word in the sentence, the context, the type of word, prefixes and suffixes, words similar to words in the mother tongue are all useful clues. Point out that students may decide to ignore some words if they do not think they are important for understanding the text. The following passage comes from *Treasure Island*. Ask students to complete the chart.

*Chapter 9*

## POWDER AND ARMS

THE *Hispaniola* lay some way out, and we went under the figureheads and round the sterns of many other ships, and their cables sometimes grated underneath our keel, and sometimes swung above us. At last, however, we got alongside, and were met and saluted as we stepped aboard by the mate, Mr Arrow, a brown old sailor, with earrings in his ears and a squint. He and the squire were very thick and friendly, but I soon observed that things were not the same between Mr Trelawney and the captain.

This last was a sharp-looking man, who seemed angry with everything on board, and was soon to tell us why, for we had hardly got down into the cabin when a sailor followed us.

| Target word | Part of speech | English meaning | Helpful items for reference |
|---|---|---|---|
| figureheads | plural noun | decoration, often in the shape of a person, at the front of a ship | ship |
| stern | | | |
| grated | | | |
| keel | | | |
| | | | |

DEVELOPING VOCABULARY

Since students acquire and store vocabulary in different ways, encourage them to develop a personal system for record-keeping. Items could be organized in their reading diaries. Suggest some of the following:

- word and translation
- word and English definition and synonym, supplemented by a picture or notes in the student's own language
- clusters: grouping of words related to: a concept or idea (for example, feeling), characters or events, parts of speech (nouns, adjectives, adverbs, etc.)

- alphabetical order
- arrangement by topic
- exemplification: writing words in sentences
- making two-sided vocabulary cards for self-testing

Point out that vocabulary work is best done after reading, so that it does not interrupt the reading itself.

USING A DICTIONARY
Each student should have access to a monolingual dictionary. Encourage students to use it for checking the meaning of a word only after they have tried to work it out for themselves. Constant use of a dictionary will interrupt reading and hinder the development of fluency. If necessary, give students some training in how to use a dictionary effectively. Explain that constant use of a bilingual dictionary encourages word-for-word translation. Encourage students to use a bilingual dictionary only after trying the monolingual dictionary.

*Practice in self-direction*
Your students may not be accustomed to making decisions about aspects of their own learning. Initially, some may need guidance when choosing books. Try to find out about their interests so you can help them select a book they will enjoy. If they have difficulties reading, suggest they try a book which contains visual support or something they may not have previously considered such as a book of puzzles or cartoons. (*See also Psychological preparation.*)

Many of the activities suggested in the Notes also provide opportunities for students to gain periods of independence from the teacher and to initiate their own activities. Essentially it is a matter of finding appropriate opportunities for relinquishing some degree of control to students.

## What to do in class: methodological approaches

*Monitoring*
Clearly, in the first instance, monitoring does mean checking that a certain amount of reading has been done and that what has been read has been understood. Monitoring should, however, become less teacher-controlled as extensive reading develops in a class and as students become familiar with the strategies and techniques of self-monitoring.

In the Notes many of the questions and tasks are specifically directed towards checking comprehension and building upon that comprehension to motivate further reading. Teacher monitoring should give way to student monitoring, for which class library record cards are useful, and for which a reading diary is also suggested.

*What is a reading diary?*

A reading diary should be kept by every student. It has the advantage of being an individual and personal record, while at the same time documenting much of the work done in class. It contains, therefore, elements of student's own monitoring as well as those of teacher-directed monitoring, for example: new vocabulary, notes made at the pre-reading stages and annotations to these throughout the reading. Students must be encouraged to use a notebook or ring-binder/folder to which material can be added on an ongoing basis. It can be arranged under several headings:

*Story:* Highlight key moments in the plot and compare expectations before reading with what actually happens. Summary skills will often be useful here.

*Vocabulary:* Keep notes of new, unusual, attractive, useful or specialized words. This will also be a useful reference resource if it is systematically organized and updated. (*See p. 9.*)

*Characters:* Make brief notes on characters to establish their relative importance in the plot, how they develop, and what happens to them in the end. Students record their own feelings or opinions about the characters, their expectations and results.

*Setting:* This can cover both time and place. Journeys and voyages can be traced; period details and descriptions jotted down and commented on.

*Narration:* Establish the narrative point of view (first person narration, third person narration, obtrusive narrator, impersonal narrator and so on). The narrative form might also be important (letters and diaries in *Dracula*, for instance). Determine the genre: fairy-tale, fable, adventure, psychological novel, fantasy, horror, animal stories and so on.

*Illustrations:* Starting with the cover, any visual material in the book can be commented on and its appositeness, contribution to the understanding of the work and enjoyment value considered.

*Style:* It is not the purpose of extensive reading to launch into stylistic or literary analysis. Students' comments on style will cover such features as archaism, humour, colloquialism, dialect, specialized language use (such as pirate language in *Treasure Island*), register and chapter length. These are the features which condition response subjectively rather than analytically. Students will often say that a book was 'easy' or 'difficult' to read largely as a reaction to a combination of any of the above elements. As their reading frame of reference grows, students will become better equipped to evaluate what made the book accessible or difficult, enjoyable or boring. This marks a move from subjective reaction to a more considered response.

Style can be seen as the overall impact of the combination of any or all of the features already listed, plus others such as lexis, syntax, phonology, graphology and so on. The stylistic 'fingerprinting' of a text is a specialized subject for analysis well outside the range and capability (not to mention interest) of most language learners.

*Mother tongue:* Obviously the reading diary will be written in the students' own language as well as partly in English. As students' language level improves, they should be encouraged to use more and more English in their reading diaries.

### Evaluation

An evaluation stage after reading is also advisable: Was the book enjoyable? Why or why not? Choose favourite or least favourite moments. Was the book easy to read? Why or why not? Could it be recommended to others? Why or why not?

### The choice and range of books

The books chosen in Part 2 (Notes) range from fables and illustrated story-books for younger learners to books which are accessible to slightly older learners at an early-intermediate level of English, and on to longer texts which will be attractive to learners with more advanced language knowledge and reading experience.

All the texts should be read as authentic, unabridged novels. Indications of age naturally refer to a school context, but adult learners are catered for in the references to years of language study. A book like *The Snowman*, with its very sophisticated graphics, can be used with classes at the earliest stages of language learning and also at much higher levels. Any risk of rejection because a book seems 'childish' can be overcome easily, even with adult learners, as the point of entry technique, outlined below, shows something of the range of involvement and interpretation in the story. Books of this kind can be seen as *bridging* books, as students move from Primary to Secondary school, or when they are introduced to extensive reading for the first time. They move from storytelling to reading, gradually increasing reader involvement, but without a dependence on the words of a text.

Stories like *Lazy Jack*, *The Very Hungry Caterpillar* and *The Mice Who Lived in a Shoe* have been deliberately included in the range because they offer a variety of possibilities for classroom interaction without being patronizing. They show *real* language in recognizable and memorable contexts, with immensely useful language-learning prompts such as the constant 'You should have . . .' every time Lazy Jack's mother scolds him. These books can be most useful at Lower Secondary level, bridging the gap between illustration-dominated stories and text-dominated novels.

The range then moves on to books where there are more words than pictures: fables retold with a modern twist, and the stories of Roald Dahl, which have universal appeal to the anarchic in every reader, young and old.

Humour plays a considerable part in enriching all these books and, as in *The Snowman*, the illustrations are very useful both as stimuli and, where there is a text, as support to the words on the page.

In the early stages of extensive reading work there will always have to be a strong degree of teacher control and monitoring. For that reason some of the texts which might be used early on (at various levels), such as *The Twits*, *Animal Farm*, *Call of the Wild* and *Robinson Crusoe*, are handled in a step-by-step way, focusing rather more on language development, plot summary and the like, while others, which might be read later, are given a more open treatment. The exercises, naturally, vary from book to book, but are generally similar in their approach.

### Bridging books and an extensive reading programme

Reading confidence and reading rhythms are built up by a progression from short texts of the kind indicated as points of entry (*see below*) or found in textbooks which develop reading skills from reading a page to a chapter, then a complete story and finally reading a full-length book.

Every reader must find his or her optimum reading speed and rhythm. These cannot be imposed, but they can be consciously developed. Bridging books are books *at any level* which take the reader a step further forward towards complete autonomy in the selection, reading and enjoyment of materials for extensive reading.

A reading programme mighr lead from *The Very Hungry Caterpillar* to *Foxy Fables* to *Animal Farm* and on to *Call of the Wild*; or from *The Snowman* to *The Witches* to *Treasure Island* and *Dracula*; from *Little Red Riding Hood* to *The Happy Prince* to *Treasure Island* and *The Adventures of Tom Sawyer*.

Bridging books can bridge from any level of ability and reading confidence to further levels and challenges.

### Who are the Notes for?
The whole class might not necessarily be reading the same book at the same time. The Notes on individual books can be used with the whole class, perhaps using a class set of a book, or with small groups, or by self-study learners reading on their own and working through the stimuli and exercises, using the cue 'discussion' for personal reflection or written work. The Notes will also be helpful for the study of extracts or short passages from the novels, either as intensive reading, or as brief introductions to the novel or author.

### How the Notes are structured
Every book has to be handled differently, so there is no rigid formula to the Notes. But some of the recurring features are:

*The Story:* This is a very brief introduction to the book. It is not intended as a proper summary but should give some of the flavour of the story and arouse reader interest in it.

*Level*: This is an indication of the appropriate class, age and language level, and of the appeal of the specific title. Clearly, some students' progress as readers, their personal interests and motivation, will sometimes take them beyond the usual prescriptive levels of what is 'suitable' at any time in their scholastic career. It is important that in the longer term students are actively encouraged to make their own reading choices based on what they *want* to read rather than on what curriculum requirements or teacher preferences dictate.

*Points of entry:* It is a good idea to have a point of entry for any extended reading text: a scene, an illustration, any paragraph or even page can be looked at or read in class before the actual reading of the whole book begins. The main criterion is for the material to be immediately accessible to the reader and sufficiently stimulating to arouse interest. It should give a starting-point (and a future point of reference throughout the reading) for all subsequent reader involvement with the text.

In general, the use of a passage as a point of entry presumes that students are already in possession of, or have access to, the book they are going to read. But, as well as stimulating the readers' curiosity by giving a flavour of the work in terms of story, characters, narration and so on, it can also help both teacher and students to select other books they feel they are more likely to enjoy reading. If three or four point of entry passages are read (they might be photocopied, or simply read aloud, perhaps with an illustration or cover picture by way of visual back-up), the class can vote for the one they like best and decide in this way what the class's next reading text will be; or separate groups can choose the passage they find most attractive and so on.

The point of entry pieces can be read largely without explanation, and the individual reader or the class should be encouraged to react to the stimuli the passage contains. Students can predict what the story will be about or express a reaction (positive or negative) to the material.

If the book is to be read by a group, or by the whole class, the teacher can then go directly to the presentation and pre-reading stimuli stage as it can be counter-productive to analyse or study the point of entry passage before coming across it in the natural course of extensively reading the book.

*Presentation and pre-reading stimuli:* This stage contains suggestions for the exploitation of various elements which lead into the initial approach to the text itself.

*Vocabulary:* A range of techniques is suggested for handling vocabulary problems. Students should be reassured that it is not necessary to understand every word they come across. They can usually ignore most new words, settling for approximate meanings, and save their energies for the more vital ones. Which words can be ignored? A simple technique is to cover or to skip the word and then see whether the sense of the whole sentence can still be understood. Encourage students not to waste time over words that are unnecessary to the understanding of the text.

*Reading:* This is handled in different ways, with indications of some problems that may arise with individual texts.

*Post-reading activities:* This is the widest range of ways to exploit texts and, naturally enough, every book has its own possibilities. None the less teachers and students should feel free to use any activity or exercise from the Notes to other books if these appeal to them.

## Flexibility

The Notes are intended to be fully flexible starting-points which teachers and students can use as they think fit for no activity is indispensable. This flexibility is the keynote to all successful teaching and learning and a great deal will depend on how much teachers and students want to check comprehension, examine formal features of the text and so on.

In general, the historical background to the books and the authors' lives have been left out of the text work to get away from the idea that reading *equals* studying. Concentration on these aspects is not part of an extensive reading programme as such and can be handled separately in a research project.

## Interaction and interpretation

Interaction with the texts read, their interpretation and discussion are actively encouraged. Students have to be stimulated to recognize the value of bringing their own expectations and experiences to bear on what they read. Opinions and interpretations *must* vary, and their exchange and evaluation is a vital part of the interactive learning process, involving language development, cultural awareness and learner growth in overall educational terms. Very often there is no one correct answer to the questions. The more open the text is to interpretation, the more rewarding it is likely to be for the reader.

George Eliot wrote in *Middlemarch* that 'all meaning lies in the key of interpretation'. Students (and teachers) who take that message to heart will become better readers not only of books but of the world they live in.

## Reading and language acquisition

Many teachers are afraid that language learning will not take place unless there is a controlled production stage. This is simply not true. Although intensive reading can help develop reading

strategies and involve students in various techniques of comprehension, reformulation and self-expression, by its very nature it
involves the close study of short passages and students' room for
manoeuvre is often limited, interaction often inhibited and the
lesson runs the risk of becoming teacher-centred. The 'explanation'
of the text by the teacher is often the thin end of the wedge.

Extensive reading offers a different kind of learning possibility
which has to be combined with intensive reading in class. It brings
together language awareness, passive vocabulary assimilation,
global rather than discrete comprehension and learner choice in
deciding how fast or how slowly to read. In short, it gives students
the freedom of the world of reading, which intensive reading
equips them with strategies to handle.

## Class library

More and more schools both in the public and the private sector are
recognizing the need for class and/or school libraries of reading
materials at all levels. In some countries these libraries constitute the
only access students have to books and their importance is fundamental to the development of reading skills and enjoyment. In other
parts of the world, while large resources may be spent on computer
or video hardware and software, there is an astonishing and
reactionary reluctance to invest in books as a resource. As current
methodological shifts restore reading to its place of primary learning
importance, this situation should be remedied. Class libraries allow
individual readers to choose the book they want to read, perhaps
after a 'taste' of the text in an extract at the point of entry stage.

### Organizing a class library

Explain the purpose of a class library to your students and try to
involve them as much as possible in its setting up and organization.
It would be inadvisable to assess your students on their class
library reading as this could cause anxiety and defeat the aim of
reading for pleasure. Also do not forget that some students enjoy
reading more than others and may already be avid readers in their
mother tongue. These will probably find reading in English easier
than the less well-read students do.

#### DISPLAYING BOOKS

It will probably not be possible for most teachers to make the
library a permanent feature of the classroom by setting up a book
corner with an attractive display of books and other relevant

17

material. If this is so, keep books in a box which is easy to move and store in a classroom cupboard. You may like to choose a class librarian(s) who can be responsible for displaying the books on a desk and packing them up. Alternatively, the librarian(s) can be elected by the class.

### CLASSIFYING BOOKS

Begin by asking students about the various types of books they read in their mother tongue. Then ask them to think about different categories of books, such as puzzles, fantasy, animals, fact books, adventure, etc. As an introductory and familiarization activity, ask students to sort the books into these categories. They could then colour code them. For example, coloured stickers could be put on the right-hand corners of the covers with red indicating fact books, black for adventure etc. so that the content of the book is clearly visible to students.

### DESIGNING A BORROWING SYSTEM

First of all, decide with the class how long books can be borrowed for. The simplest record-keeping method is to use a library lending book in which the student writes his or her name, the title of the book, the date borrowed and the date returned. An alternative system is to make a library catalogue, using a simple card index which pupils can help with. If you provide the model, students can copy it. This will provide useful study skills work: how to construct a card index, how to set out information clearly, how to place items in alphabetical order.

### Monitoring reading: using student record cards

Record cards can encourage students to keep a personal record of their reading and to monitor their progress. Suggest they complete their cards in English or in their own language at the end of each book. You may also like to look at the record cards from time to time as they will provide useful information about what books have been selected and the reading difficulties encountered.

The following items could be included on the record cards:

*Date borrowed/date returned:* to see how long it took to read the book.

*Type of book:* to encourage the student to classify the book.

*Problems:* to encourage the student to analyse any difficulties. For example if there was too much new vocabulary and if it was too difficult, or if the topic was boring etc.

## Class Library – Pupil Record Card

Name _____    Class _____

| Title/author | Date borrowed | Date returned | Type of book | Problems | Useful vocabulary and information | Comments |
|---|---|---|---|---|---|---|
| Little Red Riding Hood | 7/3 | 16/3 | Humour, modern version of traditional fairy tale. | A few words, but otherwise OK. | scatty pickles stout flurry nightie | Very funny. Good illustrations. |
| | | | | | | |

*Useful vocabulary/information:* to focus the students' attention on new vocabulary as well as on information.

*Comments:* interesting, boring, enjoyable, difficult, useful, easy, etc. These could also include comments on the use of illustrations, size of print, the cover, the title, etc. and remarks like 'I could do better next time by . . .'

## Using a class library chart

The class can be encouraged to make a class library chart which will allow students to keep a class record of the books they read. List names of students (or ask the class librarian(s) to do this) on the vertical axis and the titles on the horizontal axis. When a book has been read, the student ticks the corresponding box and marks the date. It is important to point out that this system of record-keeping is not meant to be competitive. It may be discouraging to slower readers and some students may read hurriedly, without real understanding, in order to add another tick to the chart. At the end of a term or school year, the class could write a report based on the information contained on the chart.

```
CLASS LIBRARY REPORT


Our class read _____ books this _____.

_____ read _____ books and prefers _____.

The most popular book was _____ which was read

by _____ pupils. Etc.
```

This activity will provide practice and revision of question forms. For example, 'Have you read ten books this term?', 'Do you like science fiction?'

To provide further practice in all skills, a questionnaire like the one opposite can be designed by pupils.

*Sustaining interest in the class library*

Once the class library has been introduced and set up, its aims explained, librarian(s) elected and the classification and borrowing system understood, it is important that the initial interest is sustained. Although time is limited, allow stretches for browsing and discussing books, as well as for developing reading strategies, with the class.

```
Find a classmate who

Name

_____  has read ten books this term.

_____  has read The Witches (or any
                          other title).
_____  likes science fiction.

Etc.
```

Here are some ways you can motivate students to use the class library:

i) There are almost certainly books in your class library which will provide interesting supplementary reading to a topic in your coursebook or to a news item of the week, for example, school life, the environment, pollution, humour. Draw students' attention to these and, if possible, give them a short description of the book or read a short extract to the class.

ii) Give personal recommendations from time to time on a book you have read, explaining why you liked it.

iii) Ask students to give their recommendations. For example, they could prepare a one-minute talk saying why they enjoyed a book and why they recommend it.

iv) Students can keep a reading diary in English or in their own language. Let them decide what to include: characters, events, content or story-line, the use of illustrations, the cover. It might even contain short extracts from favourite passages.

v) Students can give short, prepared readings of extracts from books they have enjoyed. You should not let the class know beforehand which book the reading is from. Pre-listening questions like the ones below can involve students actively while listening:

● What do you think the book is about?
● Which key words helped you guess?
● Who do you think are the main characters?
● When does it take place? Is it in the past, present or future? How do you know?
● What do you think the title could be?

After the reading, these questions can be discussed. Alternatively, students can ask their own questions about the extract. These activities can develop students' confidence in using English in front of an audience.

*Self-assessment*
If a cassette recorder is available, record the reading and suggest the reader listens to it afterwards for self-assessment. Students can ask themselves the following questions:

● *Pronunciation.* Did I have any problems with individual sounds, vowels or consonants?
● *Stress.* Did I have any problems with stress on individual words?
● *Rhythm.* Did I read too quickly or too slowly? Did I pause in the right places?
● *Intonation.* Did I sound interesting or boring? Did I vary the tone of my voice where appropriate?
● *Overall effect.* How well did I do? What do I need to improve?

Students usually find that recording their readings is very motivating. If the recordings are dated and kept, they can be referred to later and students can hear what progress they have made.

vi) Ask students to choose a book of the week or of the month and to produce a poster or wall display about it. This could include newspaper articles related to the topic, personal opinions, art work (such as book cover designs), letters to the author, book reviews, ideas for a sequel, ideas for a film, etc.

*Follow-up activities*
It is important that the class library also generates activity beyond its immediate purpose so that students are not left thinking, What

was all that about? Time permitting, the follow-up suggestions below provide integrated skills work for students working alone or in groups.

- Writing book reviews, summaries, questionnaires.
- Designing posters or wall displays for related work.
- Undertaking projects. For example, how to make the book into a film; researching a topic arising from it such as pollution or crime.
- Acting out role-plays. For example, interviews between author and illustrator, between author and students or between characters in the book.
- Carrying out surveys in class and with other classes on reading habits, interests, the class library, etc.
- Putting on plays.
- Recording stories or plays, complete with sound effects.
- Reading aloud, for example, stories or poetry. These readings could become part of a school open day.
- Directing a TV book programme. If possible, this could be videoed and shown to other classes and parents. Alternatively, students could make a radio book programme using a cassette recorder.
- Designing comprehension questions or vocabulary exercises for a book. These could then be used with other classes.
- Choosing a title or selected favourite extracts to be read by the whole class for intensive study.

Experience has shown that encouraging students to set up a class library and to develop their extensive reading can motivate them to read more in English, to develop independence from their teacher and to build up their confidence. Above all, it can help them to *enjoy* reading in English.

*Gail Ellis and John McRae, Pozzuoli, June 1990*

### Further reading

This brief bibliography includes a selection of useful books for teachers on aspects of reading and some suggestions for students who want to expand their reading range and skills.

Barr, P., Clegg, J. and Wallace, C., *Advanced Reading Skills*, Longman, 1981.
Bartram, M. and Parry, A., *Elementary Reading Skills*, Penguin, 1989.

Carter, R. and McCarthy, M., *Vocabulary and Language Teaching*, Longman, 1988.

Davies, E. and Whitney, N., *Reasons for Reading*, Heinemann, 1979.

Davies, E. and Whitney, N., *Strategies for Reading*, Heinemann, 1981.

Davies, E. and Whitney, N., *Study Skills for Reading*, Heinemann, 1983.

Ellis, G. and Sinclair, B., *Learning to Learn English* (Student's Book and Teacher's Book), Cambridge University Press, 1989.

Gairns, R. and Redman, S., *Working with Words*, Cambridge University Press, 1989.

Grellet, F., *Developing Reading Skills*, Cambridge University Press, 1982.

Hedge, T., *Using Readers in Language Teaching*, Macmillan, 1985 (especially Chapter 5, 'The Class Library').

McCarthy, M., *Vocabulary*, Oxford University Press, 1990.

McRae, J., *Literature with a Small l*, Macmillan/MEP, 1991.

Nolan-Woods, E. and Foll, D., *Advanced Reading Skills*, Penguin, 1987.

Nuttall, C., *Teaching Reading Skills in a Foreign Language*, Heinemann, 1982.

Smith, F., *Reading*, Cambridge University Press, 1986.

Williams, E., *Reading in the Language Classroom*, Macmillan, 1984.

# Part 2   Notes

## Section 1   Primary to Lower Secondary

### 1   THE VERY HUNGRY CATERPILLAR

*by Eric Carle*

**The story**

This is a story about growth and change. The reader is taken through the different stages of the life-cycle of a butterfly: a very small and very hungry caterpillar grows from a tiny egg to a beautiful butterfly. It is a repeating story, illustrating the use of counting and sequencing. The main idea repeated is what the caterpillar did each day: On [Monday] he ate through [one apple] but he was still hungry. This predictable pattern and the previous knowledge about butterflies allow the reader to become actively involved in anticipating the story.

The bright, colourful illustrations on double-page spreads, and cut-away pages through which the caterpillar manages to nibble his way, play an important role in aiding comprehension.

Vocabulary which comes from the story includes words from the following lexical areas: the days of the week, numbers (cardinals and ordinals), fruit, food and the life-cycle of the butterfly. The story also provides the starting-point for a variety of other related language activities which practise asking for and giving information, asking for and giving the date, asking about and expressing likes and dislikes.

**Level**

The simple structure of the book, with a beginning, a middle and an end, and the basic language provide an ideal introduction to reading for younger learners in their first year of English. Its repeating pattern resembles a rhyme which students may like to memorize and recite.

## Presentation and pre-reading stimuli

Show students the cover of the book and ask some general questions about caterpillars. For example:

- How does a caterpillar begin its life?
- What do caterpillars eat?
- How long to they stay caterpillars?
- What do they turn into next?

These questions can be asked in the students' mother tongue but should anticipate words in English like egg, leaf, fruit, cocoon and so on.

### Days of the week

Introduce or revise the days of the week by asking the date. Point out the difference between the spoken and written form. For example, we say, It's Friday, the twenty-second of June; we write Friday, 22nd June.

### True or false?

This activity provides a very simple listening and reading exercise. Give students a page from a diary and make true or false statements. For example, 'The first of June is a Monday! True or false?' Students reply, 'False. It's a Friday!' and so on.

In order to introduce On Monday, On Tuesday, ask students which days of the week they go to school, 'Do you go to school on Saturday?' and so on. This could be expanded to talking about other activities. For example, 'On Mondays, I go swimming.'

### Fruit

Ask students to tell you the name of any fruit they know in English. If possible, have a variety of pictures or flash cards that you can stick on the board as students give you these names. Introduce the vocabulary for fruit mentioned in the story – if students don't suggest it themselves – and ask them to copy pictures of the fruit into their reading diaries and to label them.

### Reading

Ask students to read the story up to 'On Friday he ate through five oranges, but he was still hungry.' You may like to read aloud and have students follow in their books. This will help convey the meaning of 'But he was *still* hungry', as you emphasize 'still'. You will probably find that your students will read aloud spontaneously with you because of the predictable pattern in this part of the story. Encourage this active participation by pausing and inviting students to join in.

After you reach Friday, ask students to tell you what the next day is and what they think the caterpillar eats. Copy the pictures of the food for Saturday from the book, introduce these words and practise the pronunciation.

The activities suggested below are designed to help students acquire the new vocabulary.

### Sorting: sweet or salty?
Mix up the pictures on a table and draw two columns on the board. Ask students to stick pictures in the appropriate column according to whether the food is sweet or salty.

### Sequencing
Give students the following instructions: put the cherry pie first, put the pickle second etc. Then ask them to arrange the pictures on the board in the correct sequence.

### Kim's game
Stick all the pictures on the board. Ask students to close their eyes and remove one picture. Then ask students to tell you which one is missing.

Returning to the book, students should read the rest of the story. If you choose to read it aloud, students will hear your rising intonation after each item as you read the list for Saturday. Ask students to say how they think the caterpillar feels that night. Then ask them to tell you what the next day is and to suggest what the caterpillar might eat. Before turning the final page, ask students to anticipate the last part of the story. They may ask you to read the story again or they may want to read it silently themselves. Encourage them to do this and allow plenty of time for them to think about the story and to ask you any questions they may have about language or content.

## Post-reading activities

### Likes and dislikes
Ask students to make their own worksheet in the form of a grid so they can interview members of the class about their likes and dislikes. Horizontally, they list different foods taken from the story or those of their choice. Vertically they write the names of people

in the class. They now interview each other. 'Do you like chocolate cake?' If a student replies, 'Yes, I do,' they tick the corresponding box or, for a negative reply, 'No, I don't,' make a cross.

## How many?

First, using the pictures Monday to Friday from the book, ask 'How many oranges are there?' Encourage the reply 'There are five oranges.' Give students a worksheet like the one opposite. Add other fruit that your students know. In pairs, students ask and answer the question 'How many . . .?' and complete their work-sheets.

## Writing

Using the diary page from the pre-reading activity, ask students to write a record of the fruit or some other kind of food they ate that week. For example, 'On Monday I ate two bananas and an apple.'

## Memory game

Ask students to work out from memory how much the caterpillar ate altogether.

## Creating stories

Students could choose another insect or animal and the food that it might eat and build these ideas into new stories of their own.

## Biology

- Students could research what different types of food caterpillars really eat.
- Students could select a butterfly or moth common in their own countries and find out about the different stages of its life-cycle, how long each stage takes, what it eats and so on. They could produce a chart, writing simple captions for each stage and labelling illustrations.

## Art and handicrafts

This story leads into a range of art and handicraft activities which could be carried out in collaboration with the art teacher:

- drawings of caterpillars and butterflies
- making models of caterpillars, butterflies and fruit.

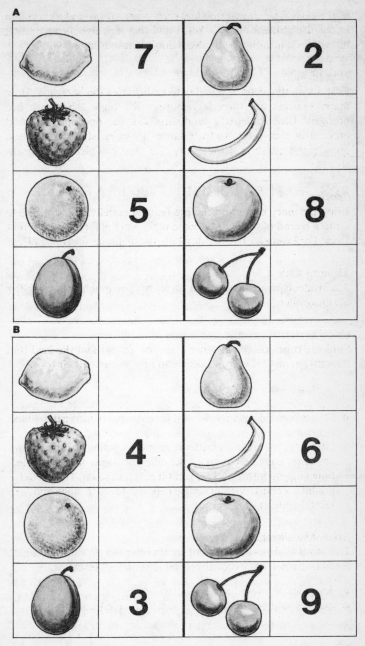

*Reciting*
As this story resembles a rhyme, students may like to memorize parts of it and recite it. Each student could learn small sections and the story could be recited around the class. Alternatively, if students work in groups of five to six, larger chunks of text can be memorized and recited.

*Notes prepared by Gail Ellis*

## 2   THE MICE WHO LIVED IN A SHOE

### *by Rodney Peppé*

**The story**
This is the story of an ingenious family of mice who live in an old shoe and who one day decide to convert it into a house. This story should appeal to younger learners in their first or second year of English. The specialized vocabulary related to house-building is easily understood thanks to the clear illustrations. The story consists of a simple narrative and conversations between the mice in cartoon-like bubble talk.

**Presentation and pre-reading stimuli**
Several pre-reading activities are suggested to introduce key vocabulary and phrases, and also to provide opportunities for students to develop their listening and speaking skills.

*Family relationships*
Ask students to look at the cover and tell you how many mice they can see. Now ask them to look at the first double-spread which gives the names of each member of the family. Introduce or revise vocabulary for family relationships. For example: grandmother/grandma, grandfather/grandpa, mother/ma, father/pa, son, daughter, brother, sister. Get students to draw a family tree (*see sample below*) featuring the characters in the story. Ask the following questions to elicit answers: 'Who is Tim?' ('Tim is Ann's brother'); 'Who is Sue?' ('Sue is Ann's sister', 'Sue is Ma's daughter') and so on. When students can ask and answer these questions confidently, they can then ask each other in pairs.

A FAMILY TREE

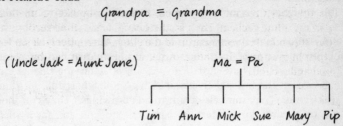

(Uncle Jack and Aunt Jane can be added to the family tree when they appear later in the story.)

EXTENSION
Students could bring in family photographs, make diagrams of their own family trees and ask each other questions: 'Who's this?' ('This is my sister', 'This is my mother') and so on.

## *The weather*
Copy the four pictures relating to the weather (second double-spread) and stick these on the board numbering them from one to four. Introduce or revise 'It's raining', 'It's snowing', 'It's sunny', 'It's windy'. Copy the descriptions from the book on to strips of paper and stick these on the board. Ask individuals to come to the board and match the description which corresponds to the picture.

## *Vocabulary*
Introduce the words dry, warm and cool (which appear later on in the book). If they wish students can draw pictures to convey their meaning.

## *Labelling*
Ask students to copy or trace on to a piece of paper the cat and the shoe illustrated on the next left-hand page. Give them the following words to label their pictures: toe end, paw, cat, shoe string/shoe-lace, hole, claws. Encourage them to label other parts of the picture too. Then draw your own picture on the board and label it. Tell students to turn over their pictures, look at yours on the board and start to play 'What's missing'. Students close their eyes and then you rub out one of the labels. Students open their eyes and tell you which word is missing. You could also rub out all the labels and give students these instructions: 'Mary, show me the toe end of the shoe', 'Andrew, show me the cat's claws' and so on.

## A dream house

Tell students that the mice decide to build a house out of their shoe, and that each member of the family draws a dream house. Refer students to these pictures and to their descriptions at the top of the opposite page. Introduce or revise adjectives and ask students to make a set of word cards with the adjective on one side and its opposite on the other. For example, big/small, short/tall, fat/thin, short/long. (They may also want to add drawings.) They can then use their cards for self-testing. Now ask students to match their descriptions to the pictures in the book.

Ask students to draw pictures of their own dream houses and then stick these on the classroom walls. Choose one and, without saying which, describe it. You may want to use adjectives the students already know or to introduce some new ones. Students must guess which house you are describing. Continue in this way until students are confident, then ask them to do the same in pairs. Finally students should choose an appropriate adjective to describe the house they have drawn and write the word beneath their picture.

## Labelling: a house

Give each student a copy of the house from the page with the words: 'The last pieces were moved in', or of the model on the last page. Put these words on the board and ask them to label their copy of the picture: wall, door, window, brick, balcony, play platform, roof. Now refer students back to their own pictures and ask them to label them.

## Reading

The key vocabulary has now been introduced. Although there will probably be other new words the students will not know, these will be understood through illustrations and mime when the story is read aloud. Where possible, vary your voice for different characters and use appropriate intonation to help convey meaning (for example, when Grandma is giving orders). The main aim at this stage is for students to understand the general meaning of the story through recognition of key vocabulary and phrases as they follow the text in their books. Interrupt your reading by asking questions or giving instructions such as 'Show me the ladder', 'Show me a tall house' and so on.

## Post-reading activities

### Making plans
– I'll build the walls
– I'll make the doors

Refer students to this double-spread. Ask them to look carefully at the speech bubbles and to tell you how the sentence structure of 'I'll make a balcony' is formed. They should be able to tell you that I'll is a contraction of I and will and that it is followed by the verb (without 'to'). Practise pronunciation.

Ask students to form groups of three to four and to choose one of the drawings of the dream houses and to decide who is going to do what job. For example, 'I'll build the roof', 'I'll get timber' and so on.

### Giving orders
– Pip, make the tea!
In the same groups as above, one student organizes his/her group and gives orders: 'David, hold the ladder!' and so on.

### Mime
Refer students to the following actions in the book:
– Pa sawed timber
– Ma held the ladder
– Grandma gave orders
– Ann mixed cement
– Mick cut the shoe string
– Mary fetched bricks

Make sure students understand the meanings by getting them to mime the actions. Ask them to find other actions by different mice. Make picture or word cards of all these. Each student chooses a card and mimes the action; the other students must guess what it is. 'You're sawing timber!' and so on.

You could also play 'Simon says'. In this game the teacher gives instructions preceded by 'Simon says' – for example, 'Simon says, "Saw timber!"' – and the students mime the action. Any instruction which is not preceded by 'Simon says' must not be mimed. Any student who mimes the action can no longer play. The game continues until there is a winner.

### Vocabulary
Ask students to look through the illustrations and make a list of the furniture and tools they see. Encourage them to use a dic-

tionary, if they do not know the English word. They may like to make a set of cards with the word on one side and its picture on the other.

*Exploiting the pictures*
Details in the pictures can be used for further vocabulary work. Give students instructions to find certain objects, for example: a blue flag, a candle, a box of matches, a ball of wool, a needle, a teddy bear and so on.

*Reading the story*
Younger learners enjoy hearing a story over and over, and so may ask you to read it again. If this is so, ask them to follow the text in their books as before, but this time to read aloud the lines spoken by the mice. You could allocate them roles.

*Notes prepared by Gail Ellis*

# 3   THE SNOWMAN

### *by Raymond Briggs*

**The story**
This is a moving yet amusing story about a boy who builds a snowman. One magical night the snowman comes alive and the two become friends. Now a classic, the tale relates well to the themes of weather, the seasons and Christmas. Its wordless story is told in a series of strip format pictures of soft muted colours.

**Level**
As the story has no text, it can be used with learners of a variety of ages and levels. They can be invited to build up the story orally or in writing by making their own interpretations of the picture narrative. As the context of each picture is very clear, the book is ideal for sensitizing learners to visual clues as aids to meaning. Predictions of what might happen next can be encouraged on almost every page.

The Notes here contain suggestions which should be suitable for students in their first three years of learning English.

### Vocabulary

Vocabulary includes items from the following lexical areas: weather, clothes, colours, parts of the body, numbers, rooms in a house, furniture, toys, escape, flying.

### Presentation and pre-reading stimuli

Do students know what a snowman is? Have they ever seen one, or maybe even made one? If they have, they can tell each other about it using these questions: 'Where were you?', 'What time of year was it?', 'Who were you with?', 'What did you use to make the snowman?', 'How did you feel?' If students do not know what a snowman is use the cover, and possibly the pages where the snowman is built, as the point of entry for the story.

Looking at the cover, ask students to describe the snowman. Is he happy or sad, cold or warm, friendly or unfriendly? Did the snowman they built look anything like this one? What other objects could be used for the nose, for eyes and so on? Do the students like snow? How did they feel the first time they saw it?

Now refer students to the back cover. Who do they think the boy is? Have they ever heard of a snowman who comes to life and can fly? Where do they think the snowman is taking the boy? What kind of story do they think it will be? Fact, fantasy, comedy or something else?

### Reading

The layout of the illustrations allows each page or double-spread to be dealt with in sequence.

### First page

Ask students to look at the first page and to tell you what is happening. They may want to begin their interpretation in this way: 'Once upon a time there was a boy called . . .' Ask students to invent a name for the boy. They may have other suggestions, all of which will be acceptable, provided they can be justified from the text. Encourage different interpretations.

The detail you go into here will, of course, depend on the level of the students. However, the main vocabulary areas would be those for clothes and for asking permission.

CLOTHES

Encourage your students to brainstorm words such as jumper,

sweater, sweatshirt or pullover, trousers or jeans and so on, and to use the word they prefer. If they are unfamiliar with these words introduce them. You could also give the words for colours and then ask students to describe the boy's clothes.

### ASKING PERMISSION

The boy is clearly asking his mother if he can go outside and play in the snow. You could introduce or revise the structure: 'Can I go outside, please?' Of course, there are other variations; encourage your students to suggest these if they have the language. The mother's reply could consist of a simple 'Yes' or it might be more detailed and include orders such as 'Don't forget to put on your boots, hat and gloves' or 'Make sure you . . .' and so on.

### LISTENING AND ARRANGING

Give each student a copy of the first page and ask them to cut up the different pictures. They put these on their desks in a jumbled order and you, or one of the students, narrate the story so far. The listeners show the pictures corresponding to each part of the story and put them in the correct sequence. (Wherever appropriate, this activity can be repeated throughout the book.)

### VOCABULARY

Each picture can be labelled and coloured for students to create their own personalized lexical sets. The pictures can then be sorted into groups and kept in envelopes. For example, one for vocabulary related to clothes, another for furniture and so on.

### First double-spread

This double-spread illustrates the process of building a snowman. At a basic level, one or two sentences could describe this. However, students can go into much greater detail. Give them the following sequencing words: first, next, then, after that, finally. Other useful vocabulary might be: scarf, hat, tangerine, coal.

### WRITING

Ask students to write instructions for building a snowman to someone who has never made one before. They may find the following vocabulary useful:

*Verbs*
to roll   to shovel   to pat   to shape   to build   to put   to lift

*Nouns*
snowball   spade   tangerine   coal   hat   scarf   buttons

They can begin: First you . . ./next you . . ./then you . . . and so on.

*Second double-spread*
Useful work can be done here on telling the time. If appropriate, students could make their own clocks. You could also give students a time dictation using a worksheet like the one here. Students ask, in sequence, 'What's the time?' You reply and students draw the hands on the clock faces.

**TIME DICTATION**

What's the time?

It's_____

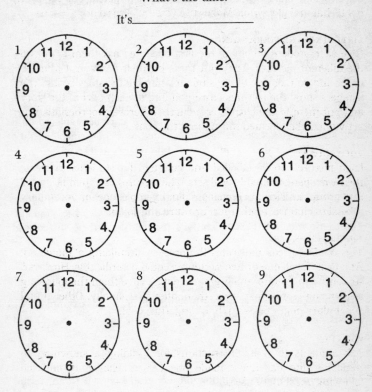

Ask questions such as: 'Why can't the boy sleep?', 'Why does he go downstairs?', 'Did you ever feel like him?', 'How do you think he felt when he opened the door and the snowman greeted him?', 'What would you do?'

*Third double-spread*

More useful language work on greetings. The snowman acts in a very formal way. What do students think he is saying: 'Hi, Hello, Good evening or How do you do? The narrative now introduces the relationship between the snowman and the boy. He invites the snowman into his house and shows him around saying, 'This is the sitting-room,' and so on. Ask students to make a list of the furniture the snowman sees, using dictionaries, if necessary. What does he like or dislike? Students could then make a list of these in two columns. For example, the snowman doesn't like the fire but he does like the cat and so on. As the boy shows the snowman around his house, students can draw a plan of it and number the rooms in the order they are visited.

*Fourth double-spread*

Here in the kitchen we see the snowman's fascination with every-day things: lights that can be switched on and off, hot and cold running water, a gas cooker, washing-up liquid, paper towels, ice cubes and a refrigerator. We learn more about the snowman's likes and dislikes. Household vocabulary can be explored and expanded here, as can exclamations such as, 'That's nice!', 'That's funny!', 'That's interesting!', 'Isn't that lovely?', and so on.

*Fifth double-spread*

Upstairs, the boy shows the snowman his parents' bedroom where the snowman dresses up in some of the father's clothes and the mother's hat. Further vocabulary for clothes can be introduced and practised here.

PICTURE DICTATION

Ask students to draw a picture of a snowman with no clothes on. Then give descriptions which the students draw. For example, 'The snowman's wearing a black hat', 'He's wearing a yellow tie', and so on.

*Sixth double-spread*

The boy now shows the snowman around his own room. Useful vocabulary for the toys is: skateboard, punch-ball, torch and balloons. The snowman is keen to try everything out, and the structure for asking permission (introduced on the first page): 'Can I have a go?' 'Can I try, please?' can be revised. 'Can' can also be introduced or revised for expressing ability: 'I can/can't skateboard', 'I can/can't box' and so on. Ask students to describe what they keep in their bedrooms.

CLASS SURVEY
Draw a chart on the board with students' names listed horizontally and their different activities written vertically (for example, skateboarding, boxing, cycling, card playing, football, windsurfing, and so on). Ask individual students the question 'Can you ride a bicycle?' One might mark a tick for 'Yes, I can' and another a cross for 'No, I can't'. Then ask students to copy the chart from the board, and to form groups of five to six for question-and-answer work on their own.

*Seventh double-spread*
Downstairs again in his house, the boy now shows the snowman the garage and we see the snowman's delight when he discovers a car and a deep freeze. Why does he like the deep freeze so much?

SORTING
Ask students to make a list of all the hot and cold things the snowman likes and dislikes. Encourage them to add ideas of their own. For example, ice-cream, frozen food and so on.

*Eighth double-spread*
Moving from the garage into the kitchen, loaded with frozen food from the freezer, the boy prepares a meal for the snowman. Useful language here would include vocabulary for food and for offering it politely: 'Would you like a (or some) . . .?'

WRITING A MENU
Ask students to write and illustrate (if possible in collaboration with the art teacher) a menu specially catering for the taste and needs of a snowman. These can be displayed on the walls around the classroom. At the end of this double-spread, ask students to say what they think is going to happen next.

*Ninth, tenth, eleventh and twelfth double-spreads*
At the ninth double-spread ask students where they think the snowman is taking the boy. If you have the audio cassette of *The Snowman* song, play this as students look at the next pages. At the eleventh double-spread ask students if they can tell you where they think the snowman and the boy are. Further details on the twelfth double-spread may provide more clues (Brighton Pavilion

and the pier). Ask students what they think the snowman is saying as he points to the sun rising. Ask them to tell you what time they think it is. Why does the snowman look worried? Why must he and the boy hurry back?

### Thirteenth double-spread
Students can write the farewell dialogue between the snowman and the boy. Bring their attention to the rising sun. How does the boy feel as he looks at the snowman from his bedroom window?

### Fourteenth double-spread
The boy finally falls asleep and then wakes up suddenly. What is he thinking? What do you notice about the light? Why doesn't the boy say good morning to his parents? What do you think the boy is going to find when he goes out into the garden?

### Final page
The snowman has melted. How do you think the boy feels? Was it all only a dream? Was it an amusing story or a sad story or both? How did *you* feel when a snowman you built finally melted? How long does the whole story last?

## Post-reading activities

### Video
If you have *The Snowman* video, show it to your students and ask them to tell you how it differs from the book.

### Christmas cards
If you liaise with the art teacher, students could make snowman Christmas cards in their art class.

### Geography
Students could compare the winter climate in their own country with the British winter.

### Collage
Students could collect pictures of hot and cold items that the snowman might like or dislike and make them into a collage.

## Creative writing

Students could write a snowman story either individually or in groups. The different versions could be put up on the classroom walls for others to read. Alternatively, students could record their own narratives on cassettes and play them to the class.

## Showing someone round your home

Ask students to draw a plan of their own home and to show a student partner around it.

## Vocabulary

Encourage students to revise the different lexical areas they have covered in the book.

## Drawing

With the art teacher's help, students could create their own stories in a series of strip format pictures inspired by *The Snowman*, or they could invent a story of their own.

*Notes prepared by Gail Ellis*

# Section 2  Lower Secondary

## 1  LAZY JACK

### *by Tony Ross*

### The story

This version of the classic fairy-tale by Joseph Jacobs is retold in a brisk contemporary style by Tony Ross and is full of bright, amusing illustrations which play an important role in aiding comprehension.

Jack is a lazy boy who spends his time doing nothing until one day his mother insists he finds a job. Near by, living in a castle, is a sad princess who does not know how to laugh. Circumstances bring the princess and Jack together.

The story contains all the elements of the traditional fairy-tale: misfortunes and fortunes, a hero and heroine, a variety of adventures and a happy ending. The repetitive element and the predictable ending enable the reader to become actively involved in interpreting the story.

The vocabulary falls neatly into the following lexical areas: food, animals, places of work and means of transportation; this allows a variety of different techniques for learning vocabulary to be introduced. Repetition of the structure, 'You should have . . .' allows useful practise in giving advice.

As fairy-tales are traditionally read aloud, this approach should be used here as part of the oral tradition. Students can follow the text as you read.

## Level

This story could be used with students at the end of their first year of English, as the illustrations provide a visual interpretation of the written text.

## Point of entry

The illustration of Jack's mother throwing a bowl at him and the paragraph beginning 'At last, Jack's mother could stand no more . . .' and ending 'You'll have to wash your own socks too' can be used to introduce students to the main character of this tale. Do students think Jack will go out and get a job? If so, where do they think he will find work? Is this a turning-point in Jack's life? Do they think he will ever change? Will he always be lazy?

## Presentation and pre-reading stimuli

### Introducing the characters

Copy and, if necessary, enlarge the following illustrations:

a) the sad princess at her castle window
b) Jack sitting in the snow and his mother carrying wood
c) Jack sitting down and his mother throwing a bowl of food at him.

Stick picture a) on the board and ask students the following questions:

- Who's this? (A princess)
- How does she look? (Sad)

To introduce or revise the words laugh and smile, ask students to tell you what happy people do. Explain that the princess doesn't know how to laugh. Stick picture b) on the board and tell students the boy is called Jack and the other person is his mother. Ask the following questions:

- How would you describe Jack? (Lazy)
- How would you describe his mother? (Hard-working)

Now stick picture c) on the board and ask:
- How do you think Jack's mother feels? Why?
- What do you think she is saying to Jack?

*Introducing the story-line*
Using pictures b) and c) ask students:
- Does Jack live in the country or in a town?
- Where could he find a job?

Elicit possible places of work and if students offer any that are in the story, list these on the board. The students may suggest places using their mother tongue and this will provide you with an opportunity to introduce these words in English. If they don't predict the places where Jack finds work, play the following game.

THE DEFINITION GAME
Give students the following definitions which they have to match with the place:

| | |
|---|---|
| a place where animals are kept and vegetables are cultivated | bakery |
| a place where sausages are made | stable |
| a place where bread and cakes are made | dairy |
| a place where horses are looked after | farm |
| a place where milk, butter and cheese are produced | sausage factory |

Ask students what kind of jobs they have done and how they were paid. Were they always paid in cash? Ask them to suggest other forms of payment for the various jobs above and to write these in, next to the place:

| Workplace | Payment/Wages |
|---|---|
| farm | _____ |
| _____ | _____ |

Ask students to copy this chart into their reading diaries.

*Transportation*
Divide the class into groups of six. Give each student a picture of the following:

- gold coin
- jug of milk
- cheese
- cat
- cake
- donkey

Each student thinks of the best way of transporting the object in their picture and mimes this to the others in the group, who must then describe what he or she is doing and guess what object is being transported. Useful vocabulary might be: 'You are carrying it in . . .', 'You are carrying it on . . .', 'You are pulling it . . .', 'I think it's a . . .', 'Is it a . . .?'

## Reading
Begin by giving the title of the story and the name of the author. Then read the story aloud and ask students to follow the text in their books.

During the first reading, the main aim is to focus on listening for general understanding through recognition of key-words and phrases, intonation and visual support. After each page, stop for students to look at the illustrations.

When you come to the penultimate double-spread, pause after 'He looked so funny . . .' and ask students to predict the ending before turning over the page. You may need to ask some questions to prompt your students. Now read the last two pages. Did anyone guess the ending?

## Post-reading activities

### Story-building
Refer students to the charts they have made of workplaces and wages. Can they remember what Jack got paid each time? Ask them to write in these wages on their original list. Get them to add another column to the chart for transportation and ask students if they can remember how Jack transported the various items. Add these to the chart.

#### WRITING: SEQUENCING
Students can now write a short summary in the following way:
– First Jack worked on a farm and was paid one shiny pound.
– Next, he . . .
Give students other sequencing words: then, after that, finally.

## Giving advice

Refer students to the book and ask them to tell you how Jack's mother gave him advice for transporting the various items.

Draw a table on the board in the following way:

| You | should | have put | it in your jacket pocket |
| You | should | have carried | the jug on your head |
| You | should | have carried | it in your arms |
| etc. | | | |

Ask students to tell you how this structure is formed.

### PAIR WORK

Again using the pictures of the objects, student A picks up a picture and student B must say 'You should have . . .' as he or she thinks of other ways to transport the items. For instance 'You should have carried it in a basket', 'You should have put it in your purse', and so on.

## Making threats

– You'll get no more meals from me!
– You'll have to wash your own socks!

Using this pattern of *will* and *the infinitive* (without to), ask students to think of five other threats they would have made if they had been Jack's mother.

## Vocabulary

A variety of different techniques can be presented for memorizing and storing vocabulary. Encourage students to write the vocabulary in their reading diaries and to experiment with the different techniques when learning other words.

### DEFINITIONS

Refer students back to the definition game (*p. 43*). Give them the following places of work and ask them to write definitions of these, using the same pattern as before: hospital, school, brewery, office, shop, post office.

Students may like to add other words of their choice.

VARIATION TO DEFINITION GAME

Students play in groups of five to six. Copy the definitions and the names of workplaces on to cards so that each group in the class has a pack. (The number of cards you make will depend on the level of your students and time available. Aim to have at least fifteen cards.) These are placed in the middle of the table. In turns, each student picks up a card and reads out the definition. The student who is able to give the place of work scores a point and the card is put aside. If no one manages to remember the name, the card is placed at the bottom of the pile and the game continues.

LEXICAL AREAS

Ask students to write down vocabulary from the story under the following headings:

| Food | Animals | Workplaces |
| --- | --- | --- |
| _____ | _____ | _____ |

CLUSTERS

Ask students to write down words they associate with happy and unhappy. For example:

| Happy | Unhappy |
| --- | --- |
| laugh, smile, funny ... | sad, cry ... |

SYNONYMS

Ask students to look through the book to find all the words which mean to say something angrily: shout, cry, screech, yell ...

WORD-BUILDING

Refer students to the word 'lazy'. Ask them what type of word it is (an adjective) and ask them to find the superlative form and the noun.

| Adjective | Superlative | Noun |
| --- | --- | --- |
| lazy | (laziest) | (laziness) |

Ask students to do the same with these words which follow a similar pattern: happy, funny, busy.

If they are not quite sure about words encourage students to check in a dictionary and also to add words of their own.

## Writing
Ask students to write short character descriptions of Jack, his mother and the princess.

## Dramatization
The story could easily be acted using these roles: a narrator, Jack, the princess, Jack's mother, the princess's parents, the employers.

## Humour
Ask students to look through the book and write down the different features that make the story funny. You may need to give some clues, for example, the illustrations, the insults, Jack's stupidity and so on.

*Notes prepared by Gail Ellis*

# 2   LITTLE RED RIDING HOOD
## *by Tony Ross*

### The Story
Like most fairy-tales, *Little Red Riding Hood* exists in many different versions and is known in most cultures in some form. The most popular is the Brothers Grimm *Little Red Cap*, but the literary history of this story begins with Perrault. It is by his title, *Little Red Riding Hood*, that the tale is best known in English. This version by Tony Ross is set in modern times.

### Level
It is likely that some students will know the story already and can make informed guesses about linguistic content and story-line. Therefore the tale can be used both by students towards the end of their first year of English, as well as by those at more advanced levels. At the lower level, more attention can be given to the linguistic content and at the higher level emphasis can be placed on the humour. The tale can also be used as part of a project to investigate the deeper meanings and importance of fairy stories.

### Style
Ross employs a colloquial style, using the simple past interspersed with short dialogues which include the famous lines: 'Oh Grandma, what big ears you've got!', 'All the better to hear you with, my

dear!' The twentieth-century vocabulary adds a delightful touch of humour, as do the excellent illustrations which support the text by giving clues to understanding.

### Point of entry
The paragraph beginning 'The little girl skipped along', and the accompanying illustration, provide good examples of Ross's contemporary style and humour. Does Red Riding Hood really think the wolf is a dog? What do students think is going to happen when the wolf opens one beady eye?

### Presentation and pre-reading stimuli
Copy the text on the first page, beginning 'Once upon a time', for each student. Ask them to read it and to try to guess which story it comes from. Encourage them to concentrate on the vocabulary they recognize. For example: little girl, forest, dad, wood, grandma, etc. Ask students with the answer to tell you what helped them guess the source. Do others agree? Did anything else help them work it out?

Now put the text and the illustration together. Does the illustration help students understand any of the unknown vocabulary? If the story has not yet been identified by some, does the illustration provide any further clues? Show students the cover illustration to confirm the title and ask them to tell you which century the fairytale is set in. Refer them back to the text and the illustration, and ask them which vocabulary and details in the illustration differ from the traditional version of the tale.

### Group discussion
Ask how many students know the story of Little Red Riding Hood and then form groups of four to five. Students who know the story then tell it to others in the group. One student should be elected to take notes under the headings suggested below and another to report back to the rest of the class.

*Main characters*     *Main events*     *Ending*

This activity will prepare students for the tale and alert them to the differences between the traditional tale and this modern retelling.

### General knowledge: fairy-tale quiz

1   Do you know who wrote *Little Red Riding Hood*?
2   Give the titles of any other fairy-tales you know.
3   Can you give the names of any authors of fairy-tales?
4   Do you know when they were written or first told?
5   What are the main features of a fairy-tale? You can discuss these aspects:
   ● they work with extreme polarities, for example, good and bad, beautiful and ugly, rich and poor
   ● the characters usually include a hero or heroine
   ● animals often behave like people, especially thinking or talking
   ● they contain supernatural elements, magic spells, fantasy (for example, a wolf cannot eat a woman and a little girl and then regurgitate them alive)
   ● they usually contain a series of events or adventures, a turning-point or climax
   ● they have a happy ending.

### Reading

The book can be divided into the following parts:

1   the first three pages: setting the scene
2   the next four pages: Little Red Riding Hood meets the wolf
3   the next three pages: the wolf puts his plan into action
4   the next five pages up to 'and collapsed on the floor in dreamy food-filled sleep': Little Red Riding Hood is eaten up by the wolf
5   the next three pages: Little Red Riding Hood's father comes to the rescue
6   the last page: the ending

Traditionally fairy-tales are read aloud and you may wish to do so. Your students can follow the text in their books. Change your voice for the different characters and also make sound-effects, where appropriate, to provide further clues to meaning. Alternatively, you may prefer your students to read the tale themselves. Depending on the time available, this reading may be done in class or by the students at home.

The approach now suggested is to check students' understanding immediately after each part, using the questions suggested below or others of your own. The aim of these questions is *not* to test students' memory, but to refer them back to the main points and details of the story. After each part, encourage students to predict what happens next in the tale. If you are reading the tale aloud, encourage students to participate by repeating key-words and phrases: for example, 'What big . . . you've got!', 'All the better to . . . you with!', etc. in Part 4.

*Part 1*
- Where did the little girl live?
- What was her Dad's job?
- Why did the little girl's Dad like her to help him?
- Did they love each other?
- How often did the little girl visit her Grandma?
- Where did her Grandma live?
- Why did the little girl's Grandma make her clothes?
- Why did the little girl become known as Little Red Riding Hood?

*Part 2*
- What were Grandma's favourite things?
- What warnings did little Red Riding Hood's parents give her before she set off on her weekly visit to Grandma's house?
- Who did Little Red Riding Hood meet in the forest?
- Why didn't the wolf eat the little girl immediately?
- What was the wolf's plan?
- What did the wolf suggest to Little Red Riding Hood?
- Did Little Red Riding Hood go straight to Grandma's?

*Part 3*
- Was Grandma expecting a visitor?
- Was Grandma happy to welcome Little Riding Hood?
- What did the wolf do when he entered the house?
- Why did he dress up as an old lady?
- Why did he turn out the light?

*Part 4*
- At about what time did Little Red Riding Hood arrive at Grandma's house?
- What four things did Little Red Riding Hood notice about Grandma?
- How did the wolf feel after he had also eaten Little Red Riding Hood?

*Part 5*
- Why was Little Red Riding Hood's father worried?

- What two things did he have with him?
- What did he do to the wolf?
- How did the woodcutter get Little Red Riding Hood and Grandma out of the wolf's stomach?
- Were they still alive?
- What did Little Red Riding Hood, her Dad and Grandma do to the wolf? Who helped them?

## Part 6

- Where did Little Red Riding Hood, Grandma and the woodcutter go?
- What happened to the wolf?

### Post-reading activities

#### Comparing and contrasting

Refer students back to the notes they took during their group discussions, based on their recollections of the traditional story. Ask them to make a second set of notes on Tony Ross's version, in order to highlight both the similarities and differences in the two stories. Does the modern version contain the features of a traditional fairy-tale?

WRITING

Now ask students to write a short text. Give them the following connectors to choose from: while, whereas, on the other hand, in contrast, however.

#### Vocabulary

Ask students to list the words and phrases in the story that show it is a modern version. The following headings may be suggested:

*Food   Entertainment   20th-century life   Colloquialisms*

#### Giving warnings

– Don't play in the traffic!
– Don't play about on the way!
– Don't lose yourself in daydreams!

Using the pattern above, ask students to give Little Red Riding Hood five more warnings.

#### Making suggestions

– Why not stay a while, enjoy the flowers and the fine sun?

Using this pattern of *why not* and *the infinitive* (without 'to'), ask students to make five more suggestions to Little Red Riding Hood.

*Verbs: the simple past*
Ask students to find the past tense of the following irregular verbs used in the story.

| | | |
|---|---|---|
| to be | to become | to feel |
| to get | to go out | to hide |
| to leap | to light up | to make |
| to put | to ring | to see |
| to sit down | to wake up | to wear |

*Dramatization*
Time allowing, students could act out this modern version of Little Red Riding Hood. They could write their own script, decide on casting, design costumes and scenery, etc.

*Discussion*
This would be for the more advanced students, to practise talking.

- Little Red Riding Hood – was an innocent and naïve little girl
  – was stupid
  – deliberately disobeyed her parents
  – was irresponsible

Discuss whether these statements are fair comment.

- Little Red Riding Hood is a cautionary tale which deliberately scares children into good behaviour. Do you agree or not? Why?
- The path of pleasure or the path of duty? Which would you have taken if you had been Little Red Riding Hood? Why?
- Do you think Little Red Riding Hood learned her lesson? Why and how?

*Humour*
Ask students to say what they find amusing about this version of *Little Red Riding Hood*.

*Fairy-tale project*
For the more advanced students you could select other tales to form part of a project on fairy-tales, investigating their stylistic

features and their deeper meanings. Divide the class into groups and give each group a different tale to study. They should report their findings to the rest of the class.

### Reading aloud

Ask students to choose their favourite extract from the story and to read it aloud, as if they were reading to a younger brother or sister. This could be done in small groups or individually. If possible, record the students so that they can listen to themselves afterwards. Give each student an evaluation sheet (*see below*) to assess their own and each other's performance. (This may need to be translated into the students' mother tongue.) Make sure the students understand the criteria to be assessed and, if necessary, provide some examples of common pronunciation errors.

| EVALUATION SHEET | | | |
|---|---|---|---|
| Points to assess | Good | OK | Needs improving |
| Pronunciation of individual sounds: vowels and consonants | | | |
| Stress on individual words and sentence stress | | | |
| Rhythm/pauses: too fast, too slow? | | | |
| Intonation: too flat? | | | |
| Overall effect: interesting? Dull? | | | |

*Notes prepared by Gail Ellis*

## 3   FOXY FABLES

*by Tony Ross*

### The story

This is a collection of six fables based on the traditional fables of Aesop, four of which feature foxes as the main characters. The other two are 'The Stag and His Mirrors' and 'The Hare and the Tortoise'. These retellings by Tony Ross are written in a contemporary style and the amusing illustrations play an important role in aiding comprehension.

## Level

Some students are likely to have read fables by Aesop or La Fontaine and will be familiar with this literary genre. However, some of the more contemporary vocabulary and phrases in these versions may be unfamiliar to them. *Foxy Fables* is therefore probably best suited for students in their third or fourth year of English, but it could be read also by more advanced students studying the literary conventions of the fable.

## Point of entry

The four illustrations from 'The Fox and the Stork' can be used to introduce students to this collection of traditional fables retold by Tony Ross. Do students find the illustrations realistic, humorous or silly? What expectations do they raise about how the fables will be told? Does anyone know this fable? Can students say what they think the moral is?

## Presentation and pre-reading stimuli

Ask students if they can give the titles of any fables they have read, name any authors of fables, and tell you where and when they were first told. Ask them to tell you who the characters usually are (animals) and what the main point of a fable is (that it has a moral). Are fables usually written in prose or verse?

Ask students to name some of the animal characters they have met in fables. If someone mentions a fox, show students *Foxy Fables* and tell them that it contains fables featuring foxes. Can they give you any titles of 'fox' fables? What are the characteristics of a fox? They may list: sly, cunning, clever, crafty, mean, danger-ous, big teeth and so on. Refer students to the blurb on the inside cover and then to the explanation about fables after the title page. Ask students to tell you what kind of changes the writer may have made to the fables for them to appeal to readers in the 1990s. You may need to ask them to consider the setting, language, illustra-tions and layout. Would the moral remain the same in the modern version, do they think?

## Reading

The fables can be read inside or outside the classroom. The class can be divided into groups and allocated one fable each or stu-dents can read all the fables. They should then give a summary of the plots to the rest of the class. Each fable is dealt with below.

## The Fox and the Crow

Refer students to the first illustration. Ask them to identify the animals: a crow, a rabbit, a rat, a snail. Ask them to describe Madame Crow and to tell you what they think she is doing. Establish that she is singing. Does she sing well or badly? How can you tell? Do students expect the text to be positive or negative about Madame Crow? Will it be serious?

Now ask students to read the first two paragraphs and to find two phrases that convey the author's attitude towards Madame Crow ('She was an unbearable crow' and 'Madame Crow was a real pain'). What made Madame Crow think she could become an opera singer? Does the situation seem comic, sad, absurd or frightening?

Ask students to read on to the end of the next page. Why do they think that the cheese stall-keeper allows Madame Crow to take the cheese without paying? The illustrations should clarify any unknown words such as cheese stall, beakful and so on. Then ask students to read the top paragraph on the next page and to cover the remaining text with a piece of paper. What do they think will happen next? Get them to uncover the text and to read on to 'and tried to impress the fox with a couple of verses of "Come into the Garden, Maud" '. Can students predict the ending? Can they also tell you what they think the moral of the fable is?

VOCABULARY

*Prefixes and suffixes* Refer students to the word, crowlet. Do they know any other words with the suffix -let? For example, piglet, booklet, cutlet, etc. What does -let mean? Does crowlet exist? Ask students to check in their dictionaries. Why has Ross used it here?

Ask students to look through the fable to find other words made up of prefixes and suffixes. For example, beakful, firmly, unaware, unbearable, etc. Then suggest that they think of some other words which use these affixes and write these down in their reading diaries. Ask them to say what difference the addition of -let, -ful, -ly, un- and -able make to the main word.

*Lexical areas* Give students the following words from the fable to sort into three groups of movement, sight and sound:

strut, walk, see, spy, stare, look, run, shout, sing, yell, screech, hop, stroll, glance, wriggle, peer

### The Cat and the Fox

Refer students to the second illustration and ask them to describe the fox and the cat and then to compare them. For example, the cat is smaller than the fox, etc. Then their personalities can be guessed at to anticipate words like: show-off, polite, pedigree, boastful, good mannered, nitwit.

After students have read the first two paragraphs ask them these questions:

- Why did the fox fall in love with the cat?
- Why didn't the cat like the fox?
- Why didn't the cat tell the fox to get lost?

Get them to close their books while you read the next part. Each time the fox boasts about something, stop reading and ask students to suggest how the cat might reply. Then refer them back to the text, to find out what the cat actually says.

Before turning over the page, ask students to suggest some of the tricks that the fox might know, and what the cat's trick could be. After they have read the rest of the fable ask them the following questions:

- Who did the cat and the fox run into?
- What did the cat do?
- Did any of the fox's tricks succeed?
- What happened to the fox?
- What was the cat's trick? Did any of the students guess it?

### The Fox and the Goat

Ask students to look at the four illustrations before they read the text. Can they tell you what happens in the fable? You may need to ask some questions which will also allow you to anticipate some of the unknown vocabulary. For example:

- Why do you think Mrs Fox has got a peg on her nose? (picture 1)
- Where are the smells coming from? (picture 2)
- How would you clear a blocked drain? (picture 3)
- Do you think the goat will fall for the trick? Why? Why not? (picture 3)

Ask students to read the first three paragraphs to answer the following questions:

● Who found the cause of the smells?
● Why did Mr Fox decide to clear the drains himself?

Then they should read the next paragraph to answer:

● Why couldn't Mr Fox clear the drain?
● Why was Mr Fox angry?

Finally the students read on to: 'There's enough smelly water for both of us'.

● What did Mr Fox say he was doing in the water?
● Why did the goat join him?

Ask students to tell you what they think Mr Fox did next. They should then continue to read until the end.

AFTER READING
Ask students to remember the three adjectives used to describe Mr Fox's personality and then to give three new ones for the goat. Do they know anyone like these animals? Ask them to tell the class about similar tricks they (or their friends) have played on 'silly goats'.

## The Fox and the Stork
Ask students to look at the four illustrations. Does anyone know the fable? Can anyone guess what happens? Ask the following questions about each illustration to elicit key vocabulary:

Picture 1
● What time do you think it is?
● They are outside a theatre. What do you think the stork's job is?
● What do you think the fox is saying to the stork?

Picture 2
● Where are they?
● What are they eating?

Picture 3
● Where are they?
● What are they eating?

Picture 4
● Who pays for the meal? Why?

VOCABULARY: ADJECTIVES

Ask students to match adjectives with their opposites in the two columns below:

| expensive | fat |
|-----------|--------|
| shallow | narrow |
| long | deep |
| thin | short |
| wide | cheap |
| tall | full |
| empty | |

(*Note:* 'short' is the opposite of long *and* tall.)

Now get students to read the fable up to the first line of paragraph two on the second page. They should then predict what happens next. What helped them guess? Repeat this technique on the next page in paragraph three, line three. Encourage the students to anticipate what happens next. Ask them to tell you which words helped them, for example, while, but. Can they tell you what they think the moral of this fable is?

## The Stag and His Mirrors

Use the suggestions below to anticipate the following words: store, paintings, handsome, fireplace, horns.

- Give another word for a shop. (store)
- What is Van Gogh famous for? (paintings)
- Give an adjective for a man who is good-looking. (handsome)
- If you want a fire indoors, where do you have it? (in the fireplace)
- Using the picture of the stag, point to his horns and ask, 'What are these?' (horns)

Ask students to read the first two pages of the story. What type of character does the stag have? Anticipate 'vain'. Ask them to look at the picture of the stag and to describe his legs. Anticipate 'thin' and 'spindly'. They should read the rest of the fable and say what they think the moral is.

## The Hare and the Tortoise

This fable is probably the best-known. Ask a student who knows it well to tell the class what happens. Ask him or her to refer to the illustrations during the explanation. Do students find the illustrations funny? Why?

Then ask students to read the first three paragraphs and ask them:

● Where are the hare and the tortoise?
● Does anyone know what the following sports are: cricket, snooker, darts, running, high jump? Can you explain them to each other?
● Why does the tortoise get angry?
● Why does the tortoise regret what he says?

Ask students to read on and to draw a plan of the race. What do they think the moral of this fable is?

VOCABULARY
Ask students to look through the fable and write down vocabulary relating to the lexical areas of sport and movement. Then have them decide which words they would use to describe the sports they practise.

## Post-reading activities

### Matching
Ask students to write the moral of each fable but not to mention the title. These are then stuck on the classroom wall and the other students guess the titles of the fables.

### Comparing and contrasting
If possible, give students copies of the original fables by Aesop and ask them to tell you what changes Tony Ross has made in his retelling.

### Human characteristics
Which of the following characteristics do the animals in the book portray?

Vanity, boastfulness, gullibility, intelligence, perseverance, cunning, stupidity, greed, superciliousness, arrogance.

Which animals in which story (or stories) display each or any of these characteristics?

## *Register*

Tony Ross uses several informal phrases. Write the following in a more formal style:

● She fancied herself as an opera singer.
● Madame Crow was a real pain.
● They looked yummy.
● The fox grabbed the cheese and gobbled it up.
● The cat was much too polite to tell the fox to get lost.
● You are such a handsome chap.
● The tortoise wished he had kept his big mouth shut.

## *Role-play*

In groups, ask students to choose a fable from the book and transform it into a dialogue, using first-person constructions. In this way, they will be encouraged to interpret the fables from different points of view.

*Notes prepared by Gail Ellis*

# 4   THE TWITS

## *by Roald Dahl*

### *The story*

Mr and Mrs Twit are a very unpleasant couple. Both are, in their own ways, repulsive: Mr Twit has a long, shaggy, bristly beard full of leftover meals (which he eats!) and Mrs Twit likes to smack animals and small children with her cane.

They enjoy playing nasty tricks on each other, but the Twits also practise on the Muggle-Wump monkeys which they keep locked up in a cage and standing on their heads. Fortunately, the Muggle-Wumps and their friend, the Roly-Poly bird, manage to plot and execute the perfect revenge.

Quentin Blake's illustrations perfectly complement this tale of two bullies.

### *Level*

The story should appeal to younger readers both in its exaggerated descriptions of the Twits and their dirty tricks, as well as in the eventual triumph of the small but clever monkeys.

## Style

Roald Dahl writes in a very colloquial, informal style; at times, the narrator seems to be trying to engage the reader in a conversation directly: 'Then there's the problem of washing. When the very hairy ones wash their faces, it must be as big a job as when you and I wash the hair on our heads. So what I want to know is this. How often do all those hairy-faced men wash their faces?' (*p. 9*). Dahl uses the present tense in these 'chats', in contrast to the simple past in the story proper. Adding to the informality is Dahl's use of made-up words, especially in moments of high emotion: 'grizzly old grunion . . . filthy old frumpet!' (*p. 41*). While this may pose a challenge to readers, it also provides a source of enjoyment.

## Point of entry

'Hey, my spaghetti's moving!' cried Mr Twit, poking around in it with his fork.

'It's a new kind,' Mrs Twit said, taking a mouthful from her own plate which of course had no worms. 'It's called Squiggly Spaghetti. It's delicious. Eat it up while it's nice and hot.'

Mr Twit started eating, twisting the long tomato-covered strings around his fork and shovelling them into his mouth. Soon there was tomato sauce all over his hairy chin.

'It's not as good as the ordinary kind,' he said, talking with his mouth full. 'It's too squishy.'

'I find it very tasty,' Mrs Twit said. She was watching him from the other end of the table. It gave her great pleasure to watch him eating worms.

This passage about the wormy spaghetti (*p. 24, l.11 to p. 25, l. 15*) is a suitably unpleasant way of introducing readers to the characters, their tricks against each other and their relationship throughout the rest of the book. What kind of people are they? How do students react to the idea of wormy spaghetti? Can they think of other similar nasty tricks?

## Presentation and pre-reading stimuli

These activities are global rather than specific, relating to the novel as a whole. The approaches to reading and vocabulary described under the heading Reading will in fact contain some activities which could be done *before* reading a specific chapter or section of the book, but which represent or exemplify strategies which may be used on an ongoing basis.

*Looking at the book for the first time*

If students don't know what 'twit' means, they should be encouraged to look the word up in a dictionary. Ask them to describe the people on the cover. What can they guess about their personalities? And what do they think about the setting of the book? Have them compare guesses with a friend.

The Contents page gives the titles of all the chapters. After reading through them, the students might want to add details to the above descriptions. Ask students to look through the illustrations in the book. See whether they can match any of the illustrations to chapter titles (for example, 'Mrs Twit Gets a Stretching' (*p. 34*). The illustration on the facing page will help explain what 'Gets a Stretching' means and will also give an idea of what goes on in the book. Similarly, the next chapter, 'Mrs Twit Goes Ballooning Up' (*p. 36*) is illustrated in the drawing on p. 37. The teacher may like to point out that the verb phrases used here are *not* standard English, but typical of Dahl's colourful style.

The back cover can also be examined. Ask students how they think the monkeys will fit into what they have seen so far. Why are they in a cage? Why are they upside down?

*Dirty tricks*

Since the two major threads of the story relate to nasty tricks played by the Twits (on each other and on others) and to the revenge of the Muggle-Wump monkeys, the students can be sensitized to the issues by the following questions, to be discussed in pairs or small groups:

● Has someone ever played a trick on you? Describe it.
● Did you get your revenge? If so, how?

**Reading**

The novel can be divided into five sections:

● 'Hairy Faces' (*p. 9*) introduces the subject of beards.
● The next three chapters (*pp. 10–16*) introduce the Twits, and are mostly descriptive.
● The next nine chapters (*pp. 17–43*) describe a series of episodes in which Mr and Mrs Twit play nasty tricks on each other.

● The next eight chapters (*pp. 44–64*) introduce the Muggle-Wump monkeys, the Roly-Poly bird and Hugtight Sticky Glue. These chapters add further detail to the Twits' characters, and also help to prepare the scene for the revenge that befalls them.
● The last eight chapters (*pp. 65–95*) describe how the Muggle-Wump monkeys, the Roly-Poly bird and other birds use Hugtight Sticky Glue to get revenge on the Twits and make a final escape.

*Getting started*

The teacher can introduce the first chapter with the word cluster activity described in Vocabulary (*See Post-reading activities, p. 67*).

PRE-READING QUESTIONS

● Do you know anybody with a beard?
● What are some of the reasons men grow beards?
● Do you like beards? Why or why not?

The teacher can read the first chapter aloud while students listen and follow in their books before answering the following questions:

● What is this chapter about?
● Does the book seem serious or humorous so far? Explain why you think so.

*Meeting the Twits*

Words from this section can be jumbled and put on the board:

fearful, grand, hairy, horrid, lovely, revolting, smelly, ugly, wise.

Ask students which words describe Mr Twit? And Mrs Twit?

*Dirty tricks*

The actual narration begins in this section, in a series of episodes which begin with Mrs Twit playing a trick on Mr Twit, initiating revenge, counter-revenge and so on.

The Twitgraph below is aimed at encouraging students to respond independently to the text as they read. The graph will show the relationship between the Twits (how one cannot be happy if the other is), and the note-taking is structured to give summarizing practice and to develop a responsive, questioning attitude towards the text. The Twitgraphs can be filled in for homework to provide a basis for comparison with others in class discussion. Or it can be used as an end-of-lesson activity to help students keep an organized record of what they have learned.

INSTRUCTIONS TO STUDENTS

As you read this section of *The Twits*, keep a chart of the feelings of Mr and Mrs Twit. *Good*, *positive* feelings (like happiness and excitement) go on the top half of the graph (the *best* feelings go on the very top line), and *bad*, *negative* feelings (such as anger, shock or horror) go on the bottom half.

'The Glass Eye' (*p. 17*) has been done for you.

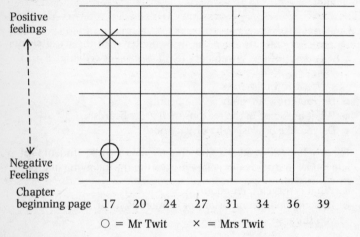

| What happens | Comments, questions |
|---|---|
| *Mrs Twit leaves her glass eye in Mr Twit's beer glass. He drinks his beer and finds it there. It's a nasty surprise for him (−), but Mrs Twit thinks it's funny (+)* | *Mrs Twit is really horrible! I wonder what Mr Twit will do.* |

Keep notes on *what* caused their feelings, as well as your own comments and questions.

### Introducing the other characters

**'The House, the Tree and the Monkey Cage'** (*pp. 44–6*)
The picture of the Twits' house and garden could be put on a transparency and students asked to write short descriptions of what they see especially noting anything strange or odd. For example, there are no windows in the house. Students should also include a brief discussion of *why* they think these oddities exist: 'The Twits' house has no windows. This is because they are too mean to spend extra money on glass.' Students can then skim the chapter to see if their guesses were correct. The aim here is to give practise in the strategy of 'guessing ahead and checking'.

Students can be encouraged to speculate:

● What will happen next?
● What do the monkeys have to do with the story?

**'Hugtight Sticky Glue'** and **'Four Sticky Little Boys'** (*pp. 47–51*)
What do we learn about Mr and Mrs Twit in these chapters? (They eat birds, they use glue to catch them, they can be outsmarted.) How do the little boys escape? Because glue is going to be very important in the final section of the book, students could focus on the uses of Hugtight Sticky Glue by writing an advertisement for it, with a testimonial by Mr and Mrs Twit.

(*pp. 52–64*)
The Twitgraph can be used in the subsequent chapters if the additional characters, Muggle-Wump and the Roly-Poly bird, are plotted in. A difference between this Twitgraph and the previous one may be noted by the students or elicited by the teacher. When the Twits are by themselves only one can be happy at a time, but when they are teamed up in opposition to a common 'enemy', their feelings are the same.

### Revenge
The last chapter of the previous section ends with the Twits going off to buy guns. Before beginning the final section, students can be asked the following:

● What are Mr and Mrs Twit going to do now? Why?
● What do you think the animals ought to do?

Students can scan 'Muggle-Wump Has an Idea' (*pp. 65–8*) to see whether their ideas match Muggle-Wump's. They can then be asked *how* Muggle-Wump plans to turn the Twits upside down.

Discussion here should be specific. Presumably, Hugtight Sticky Glue will be used, but how?

(*pp. 69–82*)

The next three chapters are especially notable for their excitement and action. These are conveyed by short exclamatory sentences and lots of 'action' verbs. (In addition, the other animals seem to think that Muggle-Wump has gone crazy.) The same listening-while-reading procedure can be used as for Getting started (*p. 63*) with students listening and following in their books as they consider the following:

● What feelings are expressed in these chapters and by whom? (These can be selected from a list written on the board, if necessary; the list should include: excitement, horror, glee, scepticism and so on.) Ask students to justify their answers based on what they have heard and read.
● How do the animals react to Muggle-Wump's plan?
● Why do students think he wants to put everything on the ceiling?

*Conclusion (pp. 83–95)*

Ask students to look at the illustration on p. 84 and to answer the following:

● What is happening here?
● Why is this important?
● What will happen next?

Students scan the 'The Ravens Swoop Over' (*pp. 83–5*) to confirm or modify their guesses.

Students then look at the following jumbled sentences, which summarize the ending of the book, and put them into the correct sequence (shown by the numbers in brackets).

a) The monkeys find out how cold English winters are. (3)
b) Everyone shouts 'Hooray!' (6)
c) The Twits go inside the house. (1)
d) The Roly-Poly bird offers to take the monkeys home. (4)
e) The Twits stand on their heads. (2)
f) The Twits get the Dreaded Shrinks. (5)

Discussion: Did the Twits get what they deserved?

### Post-reading activities

*Quiz programme*

Working in teams, students prepare sets of questions (and correct answers) about the story. Once these are compiled, one student acts as quiz-master, another as score-keeper and another as time-keeper. (Rules, timing and other conditions will naturally vary according to local needs and constraints.) Teams then play against each other.

## Questions
Students can be encouraged to write out genuine queries (those they really do not know the answers to) and to put these in a box at the front of the classroom. The aim here is to encourage a questioning attitude towards the text, as well as to provide feedback for the teacher about misunderstandings and misapprehensions.

## Literary consequences
This activity aims to encourage students to analyse the consequences of specific actions in the story. It can be used as an ongoing activity or for revision.

A factual statement is given (for example, the Muggle-Wump monkeys were forced to stand on their heads all day long) and then the question is asked, 'And the consequence was . . .?' (Immediate consequence: they felt very uncomfortable; longer-term consequence: they decided to seek revenge.)

## Quotations
The teacher (and/or students) collect a series of quotations from the book (or from specific sections) and others are asked to identify the speaker, the situation and the importance of each quotation.

## Word search
This can be done as a revision activity or it can be filled in as students read the book.

*Instructions:* The following sentences review (*p. 68*) events in the book, but in each sentence a word has been omitted. Find the word and fill in the blank.

A worksheet for the use of students (which you can photocopy) is on p. 73.

## Vocabulary
Suggest that students note down new vocabulary in their reading diaries.

### CLUSTERS
The aim of this type of exercise is to help students focus on groups of words which are in some way related to one another, in a specific chapter or throughout the book.

1 Mr Twit had a thick, bristly _____ (beard).
2 Mrs Twit thought that a _____ was going to bite her nose (skillywiggler).
3 She made Mr Twit some spaghetti that was made of squiggly wiggly _____ (worms).
4 Not long after, she 'fell ill' with a mysterious disease called the _____ (Shrinks).
5 To stretch her, Mr Twit used _____ that made Mrs Twit float up in the air (balloons).
6 The Twits liked to eat bird ___ for supper once a week (pie).
7 Mr Twit spread _____ glue to catch the birds (Hugtight).

8 The _____ bird came to the rescue of the monkeys (Roly-Poly).
9 Unfortunately, when the glue didn't work, Mr and Mrs Twit decided to buy some big, loud _____ (shotguns).
10 While they were out shopping, the monkeys and their friend decided to play a _____ on the Twits (trick).
11 They glued everything in the Twits' house to the _____ (ceiling).
12 The animals escaped and Mr and Mrs Twit got the Dreaded Shrinks and _____ (disappeared).

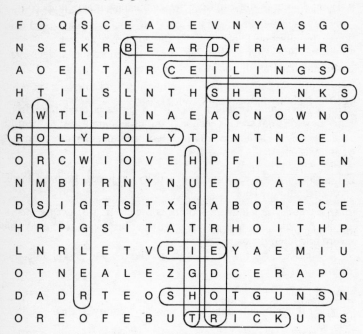

Before reading chapter 1, 'Hairy Faces', students are asked to brainstorm for five minutes to think of all the words they know that are related to *hair*. As they call out words, the teacher puts them on the board and students copy them into their reading diaries.

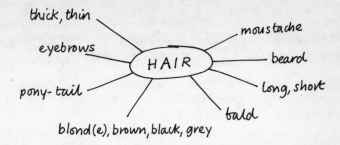

Words suggested by one student which are unfamiliar to others can be defined by the student or clarified by the teacher. The teacher can also anticipate unfamiliar 'hair' words in the text by asking:

- What do men comb into their hair to make it smooth and shiny? (hair tonic)
- Whose job is it to cut hair? (barber – a 'giveaway')
- What is the difference between 'cut' and 'trim'? (a 'cut' takes off more than a 'trim')

Students can refer to the cluster as they read and tick off the words which actually appear in the text. They can add to their list of 'hair' words in chapters 2 and 3 (*pp. 10–13*).

Students could build up lists of words related to:

- animals and their characteristics
- reporting verbs (said, cried out, screamed and so on)
- 'nasty' words (foul, smelly, ugly, and so on)

These three categories are found throughout the book and could be added to as students read on. If students have any difficulty, these additions could be done as a class activity on a large wall-chart, with different students responsible for different sets of words.

### REAL OR INVENTED?

This exercise contrasts the genuine with the made-up words in the novel. Give students the following list of words, all taken from *The Twits*. See how many of them can correctly identify which words are real and which have been invented by the author (Hint. There are eight real words, which can be identified by completing the crossword puzzle):

froth, frumpet, gnosh, grunion, hugtight, maggoty, muggle-wump, nitwit, skillywiggler, slashed, squishy, swazzle, weird, wombat, wonky.

The completed crossword puzzle follows. (You can make copies of a blank crossword grid for the students' worksheets.)

*Plan the movie*
Students work in groups to plan a film version of *The Twits*. They must decide:

● which episodes to include (isolating main from subsidiary events)
● which actors will play the main roles (making inferences about characters; matching character interpretation to real-life people)
● where the film will be set (matching fictional setting to a real-life one)

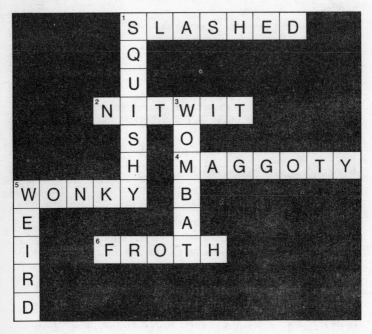

**Clues across**
1 Cut; made cutting motions (7 letters) (slashed)
2 Idiot; brainless person (6 letters) (nitwit)
4 Full of worms (7 letters) (maggoty)
5 Crooked; not quite straight (5 letters) (wonky)
6 Foam found on top of beer (5 letters) (froth)

**Clues down**
1  Unpleasantly soft (7 letters) (squishy)
3  Australian animal (6 letters) (wombat)
5  Strange; peculiar (5 letters) (weird)

*Writing*

REPORTS

A simple form (*see next page*) can be used to help students summarize important events in the story.

DIARY ENTRIES

Alternative points of view can be explored by having different groups of students take different characters' roles and write diary

---

Report on:_____

Who was involved?

_____

_____

What happened?

_____

_____

_____

---

entries describing the same event. For example, Mr Twit and Mrs Twit and one of the monkeys can write their own versions of 'Mrs Twit Comes Ballooning Down'.

PREQUELS AND SEQUELS

A variety of writing topics can be generated from two questions:

● What happened before the story took place?
● What happened after the story ended?

In either case the student must present new information but match it to the text's register, vocabulary, characterization, style, etc.

Possible ideas (to be done individually or in groups):

- Describe Mrs Twit as a little girl. Was she nasty or nice? Did she have any friends? What games did she like to play? How did she behave at school? How did she get her glass eye?
- Mr Twit did not always have a beard. Write a short story which explains why he decided to grow one. Did he have a skinny neck to hide? Did his future wife ask him to?
- The Roly-Poly bird likes to travel to foreign countries. Describe his visit to somewhere you know. When did he go? What did he do? Who did he meet?
- The Muggle-Wump monkeys escape from the Twits' monkey cage and go home to Africa – one by one – on the back of the Roly-Poly bird. Write a letter from one monkey to another about the journey home.
- What happens to the Twits' house and garden after they disappear? Does it become haunted by their ghosts? Do the neighbours decide to tear the ugly house down and build a new one? Do the small boys make it into a clubhouse? What would *you* do?

*Linking activities*

Some of the pre-reading activities can be quickly 're-visited' and compared with students' final impressions of the story:

- The definition of 'twit': *The Penguin English Students Dictionary* defines the word 'twit' as 'stupid person'. Are the Twits really twits? Or something different? What might be a better name for the Twits?
- The Contents page: students can look back at the chapters they thought would be most interesting. Were they as good as anticipated or were there other chapters that were more intriguing?

*Dramatization/mime*

This activity provides opportunities for revision, fluency and pro-nunciation practice, as well as for a close reading of the text, especially with regard to characterization.

The teacher chooses a set of short extracts from the story to be dramatized by students working in groups. Students divide roles and make decisions about how the character *behaves* and *sounds* (gruff or squeaky, slow- or fast-talking, etc.).

*Discussion*

Although *The Twits* is not a serious book, it does raise some serious questions about human behaviour:

● In some schools bullying is a serious problem. What is the best way to stand up to a bully: violently or non-violently? Should teachers and parents be involved, or should students handle such problems themselves?

● 'Mrs Twit wasn't born ugly . . . The ugliness had grown upon her year by year as she got older' (*p. 14*). Although *The Twits* is a highly fantastical story, Mr and Mrs Twit may remind you of people you know in real life. What causes people to act like the Twits? Can 'the ugliness' be prevented or stopped, or is it unavoidable?

● How do you suppose the Muggle-Wump monkeys got captured by the Twits? Why didn't they ever try to escape? Again, do you know people like the Muggle-Wumps who seem to be natural *victims* for bullies?

Students may prefer to pose additional questions for discussion with other groups.

WORD SEARCH

| F | O | Q | S | C | E | A | D | E | V | N | Y | A | S | G | O |
|---|---|---|---|---|---|---|---|---|---|---|---|---|---|---|---|
| N | S | E | K | R | B | E | A | R | D | F | R | A | H | R | G |
| A | O | E | I | T | A | R | C | E | I | L | I | N | G | S | O |
| H | T | I | L | S | L | N | T | H | S | H | R | I | N | K | S |
| A | W | T | L | I | L | N | A | E | A | C | N | O | W | N | O |
| R | O | L | Y | P | O | L | Y | T | P | N | T | N | C | E | I |
| O | R | C | W | I | O | V | E | H | P | F | I | L | D | E | N |
| N | M | B | I | R | N | Y | N | U | E | D | O | A | T | E | I |
| D | S | I | G | T | S | T | X | G | A | B | O | R | E | C | E |
| H | R | P | G | S | I | T | A | T | R | H | O | I | T | H | P |
| L | N | R | L | E | T | V | P | I | E | Y | A | E | M | I | U |
| O | T | N | E | A | L | E | Z | G | D | C | E | R | A | P | O |
| D | A | D | R | T | E | O | S | H | O | T | G | U | N | S | N |
| O | R | E | O | F | E | B | U | T | R | I | C | K | U | R | S |

1 Mr Twit had a thick, bristly _ _ _ _ _.

2 Mrs Twit thought that a _ _ _ _ _ _ _ _ _ _ _ _ _ was going to bite her nose.

3 She made Mr Twit some spaghetti that was made of squiggly wiggly _ _ _ _ _.

4 Not long after, she 'fell ill' with a mysterious disease called the _ _ _ _ _ _ _.

5 To stretch her, Mr Twit used _ _ _ _ _ _ _ _ that made Mrs Twit float up in the air.

6 The Twits liked to eat bird _ _ _ for supper once a week.

7 Mr Twit spread _ _ _ _ _ _ _ _ glue to catch the birds.

8 The _ _ _ _ _ _ _ _ bird came to the rescue of the monkeys.

9 Unfortunately, when the glue didn't work, Mr and Mrs Twit decided to buy some big, loud _ _ _ _ _ _ _ _.

10 While they were out shopping, the monkeys and their friend decided to play a _ _ _ _ _ on the Twits.

11 They glued everything in the Twits' house to the _ _ _ _ _ _ _.

12 The animals escaped and Mr and Mrs Twit got the Dreaded Shrinks and _ _ _ _ _ _ _ _ _ _ _.

## VOCABULARY: REAL OR INVENTED?

**Clues across**

1 Cut; made cutting motions (7 letters)
2 Idiot; brainless person (6 letters)
4 Full of worms (7 letters)
5 Crooked; not quite straight (5 letters)
6 Foam found on top of beer (5 letters)

**Clues down**

1 Unpleasantly soft (7 letters)
3 Australian animal (6 letters)
5 Strange; peculiar (5 letters)

*Words to choose from*

| | | |
|---|---|---|
| froth | frumpet | gnosh |
| grunion | hugtight | maggoty |
| muggle-wump | nitwit | skillywiggler |
| slashed | squishy | swazzle |
| weird | wombat | wonky |

*Notes prepared by Marti Sevier*

## 5 CHARLIE AND THE CHOCOLATE FACTORY

### by Roald Dahl

### *The story*

This is an almost surrealistic adventure story about five children. There is a moral overtone: the four bad children are made to mend their ways and get no more than they deserve, and the one good child is justly rewarded. The story is in Roald Dahl's familiar zany and action-packed style. Students may find his rich

vocabulary and linguistic inventiveness a little off-putting initially, but they should be strongly encouraged to get the gist of
the story.

Line drawings of most of the characters and scenes illustrate the
text, which is also interspersed with fairly long and amusing
moralistic rhymes. The book lends itself to dramatic readings in
class, particularly the chapters about the winners of the Golden
Tickets and the adventures in the factory. A dramatic adaptation,
with hints for staging the play, by Richard George, is also published
by Puffin.

### Level

The story would have great appeal for early learners. It is best
suited for students in their third or fourth year of English.

### Point of entry

> In the town itself, actually within *sight* of the house in which
> Charlie lived, there was an ENORMOUS CHOCOLATE
> FACTORY!
> Just imagine that!
> And it wasn't simply an ordinary enormous chocolate factory,
> either. It was the largest and most famous in the whole world! It
> was WONKA'S FACTORY, owned by a man called Mr Willy
> Wonka, the greatest inventor and maker of chocolates that
> there has ever been. And what a tremendous, marvellous place
> it was! It had huge iron gates leading into it, and a high wall
> surrounding it, and smoke belching from its chimneys, and
> strange whizzing sounds coming from deep inside it. And outside
> the walls, for half a mile around in every direction, the air was
> scented with the heavy rich smell of melting chocolate!

This extract (*p. 18, ll. 10–23*) can be used to arouse interest in the
factory, its location and what students imagine it might look like.
Comparisons could also be made with the cover illustration. Which
image do students prefer: the visual or the written? Why?

### Presentation and pre-reading stimuli

#### Setting the scene

Ask students to read the first paragraph of the blurb on the back
cover. Check that they understand what a factory is. Ask them if
they have ever visited one and, if they have, to recount the
experience to the class (or a partner, if many students respond).
Discuss whether it was an enjoyable experience or not, whether

factories are pleasant places to work, whether people earn much money in them, and so on. Students make notes on these points for later use.

Now ask students to study in detail the picture on the front cover. Elicit how it differs from their ideas of factory life (for example, colour, nature). Ask them to imagine and describe an ideal factory or to draw one. (This could be set up with the art teacher.) The descriptions and drawings can be as fantastic as the students like.

Finally, ask them to imagine what adventures (pleasant and/or unpleasant) and 'accidents' could happen in their imaginary factories.

*Language preparation*
There are many words to do with eating in the book, some of which can be anticipated as follows:

● Copy these two lists on the board and ask students to draw lines between the way of eating with the type of food. Explain that there may be more than one answer. They can use their dictionaries or you can mime the different ways of eating before the students begin.

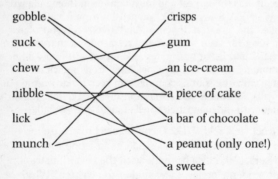

● Other food vocabulary (much of it on *p. 22*) could be incorporated into a questionnaire about food and eating customs or habits. This could be done as pairwork. Here are some examples:
   – Give three types of food that you would refuse to *taste*.
   – Give three types of food that *make your mouth water*.
   – Which is worst: being *lazy*, *selfish* or *greedy*?
   – In what parts of the world are people *starving*?

## Reading

### Chapter 1  Here Comes Charlie

Check that students have grasped the relationships (perhaps by drawing a family tree) and the daily routine of the different members of the family. You can draw a page of a diary on the board and ask pupils to fill it in like this:

8 a.m.    *Mr Bucket goes to work in the toothpaste factory.*

8.30 a.m. *Charlie leaves for school.*

12 noon   *Grandparents still in bed !*

Have a brainstorming session on luxury and essential food (two columns on the board).

### Chapters 2–4  Grandpa Joe Relates the Story of Mr Wonka's Factory

MR WONKA'S INVENTIONS
Write the following statements about the inventions on the board. Are they true or false? (*p. 22*)
● Ice-cream that doesn't need to be kept in the freezer. (*T*)
● Chewing gum that changes its taste several times as you chew it. (*F*)
● Sugar eggs with real birds inside them. (*F*)
● Sweets that taste of flowers. (*T*)
● Sweets that get larger. (*T*)

THE INDIAN PRINCE
Imagine you are the Indian Prince. What other extraordinary things could you ask Mr Wonka to make out of chocolate? Choose the three best ideas in the class.

To cope with the vocabulary on houses, students can label the picture on p. 25 or they can make their own plan of the palace and label it.

THE SECRET WORKERS
Check that students understand the example of 'industrial espionage'. Ask them to give examples of secret technologies from other industries (the car industry for latest developments; new types of audio-visual equipment etc.). How do 'normal' industries cope with spying, without going to Mr Wonka's extravagant measures of keeping the factory completely closed to people? (Security, patents and so on.)

Who do students suppose the 'tiny people' could be? Where do they think Mr Wonka found them?

## SUMMARY WORK

Students write the story of Mr Wonka's factory in 150 words. They swap their summaries with a partner and reduce each other's summaries to 100 words. They check with the original writer of the summary that nothing essential has been left out. They swap summaries with another partner and reduce them to 50 words. Some of the summaries are read out in class or written on the board. Does the class agree on the essential elements of the story so far?

## Chapters 5–12  The Golden Tickets

### PREDICTING

Once the idea of the competition has been understood, ask students to predict what kind of children the winners are by looking at the drawings on pp. 33, 36, 42 and 44. Elicit the notion of spoilt children.

### ROLE-PLAY

Divide the class into five groups. Each group chooses one of the children and role-plays the interview between the journalists and the child who has just found a ticket. You can prepare the type of questions the journalists would ask before you begin. The interviews can then be written as sketches and acted out to the whole class.

### SUMMARY WRITING: Spot-the-mistake summaries

Divide the class into five groups. Ask each group to write a summary: Group 1, chapters 5 and 6; Group 2, chapter 7 (this is shorter and easier, so you could choose a group of weaker students to do this); Group 3, chapter 8; Group 4, chapters 9 and 10; and Group 5, chapters 11 and 12. Students must include five errors in their summary and should make four copies of it. Then each group gives a copy of its summary to the other groups who find the errors without referring back to the book. Have a bar of chocolate ready as a prize for the group which spots all the mistakes first!

### WRITING

Ask students to imagine they are the foreign correspondent of a newspaper which has just heard about the chocolate factory story. Write the story so far, highlighting the dramatic elements to make a good newspaper story of less than 200 words.

PAIRWORK (or small groups)
Think of a suitable 'punishment' or fate for each of the revolting four winners!

## Chapter 13  The Big Day Arrives
This chapter lends itself especially to a dramatized reading. Encourage high–low intonation patterns for expressing excitement and for exclamations.

## Chapter 14  Mr Willy Wonka
Before you read the chapter, ask students to describe Mr Wonka in detail from the front-cover illustration. They can check themselves by reading p. 64.

Before you get to the passage about smells on p. 70 brainstorm the class's favourite smells.

## Chapter 15  The Chocolate Room
Ask the students to turn to the notes they made at the beginning (*Setting the scene p. 75*) about life in a factory. While they read this chapter, ask them to make a parallel list about life in Mr Wonka's factory.

## Chapter 16  The Oompa-Loompas

SUMMARY WRITING
Write the next chapter in the story of Willy Wonka's factory (*see chapters 2–4*).

DISCUSSION
How moral is Mr Wonka's action of bringing people back to live in captivity – even if the conditions are wonderful? This is the 'golden-cage' phenomenon. Can you think of other examples in life of people who sacrifice their freedom for a pleasant life-style? (Perhaps those who have boring jobs in large bureaucratic organizations, some married women who do not work and have wealthy husbands and so on.)

## Chapters 17–27 The Visit

After Augustus Gloop's 'accident', ask students to predict the fate of the other children.

These chapters are about a journey round the factory (which really begins in chapter 15). Ask students to keep a graphic record of it, drawing in each scene as they go along (with the cooperation of the art teacher, if possible). They can do a drawing or a plan, labelling as much as possible of each of the different processes going on in the factory.

Ask students to make a list of all the different sweets made in the factory. In groups of three, they decide which is the best, giving reasons for their choice. They make three more suggestions for Mr Wonka to manufacture in the future.

### SUMMARY WRITING

Following the suggestions for chapters 5–12, this time divide the class in four groups, each writing about what happened to one of the children.

### PRONUNCIATION WORK

Ask students to work out the rhythm in the rhymes on pp. 86, 108, 125 and 145 and mark in the 'beats'. Different groups can work on different rhymes. The students will become more aware of the stress system in English.

> Dear friends, we surely all agree
> There's almost nothing worse to see
>
> Than some repulsive little bum
> Who's always chewing gum.

Each group reads their rhymes out to the rest of the class, each member of the group reading a couplet at a time.

## Chapters 28–30 Charlie Wins the Chocolate Factory

### PREDICTING

Will the four children be all right in the end? What will happen to Charlie?

### WRITING

Half the class should write the foreign correspondent's second dramatic article, recounting how Charlie became owner of the chocolate factory (see chapters 5–12). The other half should write the third part of the story of the factory (see chapters 2–4 and chapter 16). In pairs they compare what they have written. Is there a difference? Is one really dramatic? Is one really 'history-book' style? Students improve the two texts to make them stylistically different. (The emphasis will be mostly on the choice of adjectives and adverbs and possibly in the order in which the events are related.)

## Follow-up

### Remembering the story

● Jumble the Contents page and ask students to put the chapters back in order. They correct each other's lists before checking in the book.

● In groups of four or five, one pupil mimes one of the characters from the story. The others guess who it is, explaining how they guessed. The best mimes are done in front of the whole class.

### Morals

Which of the following morals would you choose for the book? You may also invent one of your own.

● Every cloud has a silver lining.
● People always get what they deserve in the end.
● Good is stronger than evil.

### Vocabulary

SYNONYMS

Roald Dahl uses many words to express one idea. Ask students to do some research on this, showing them this example on p. 101: machine noises – rumbling, hissing, sloshing, splashing, whizzing, whirring.

The point of this exercise is to sensitize students to the idea that there are many different forms of expressing the same idea. It also shows one of the ways in which Roald Dahl obtains exaggerated stylistic effect. Do not do any precise vocabulary work on slight differences of meaning as it would be inappropriate at this level. Just listing words with similar meanings will lighten what might appear as a very heavy vocabulary load in certain parts of the book.

Other word groups are: words and phrases for tastes good in chapter 2 (sweet, creamy, delicious, melts in your mouth); words and phrases for feeling shock on p. 56 (dizzy, floating sensation, feet not touching the ground, heart thumping); words for surprise on p. 74 (flabbergasted, staggered, dumbfounded, bewildered, dazzled, bowled over); words for being mad on p. 93 (balmy, nutty, screwy, batty, dippy) and so on.

PLAYING WITH WORDS

Roald Dahl enjoys word-play. Study the examples for 'cream' and 'whipped' on p. 34; 'has bean' ('has been' someone whose life is not as successful as it was before) on p. 35; 'round' on p. 116. A particularly creative class might be able to begin punning in this way. Start by suggesting a few homonyms, for example, a note (musical, bank note, message); a cape (toreador's and a promontory); a line (telephone line, railway line, line on a page).

ASSOCIATIONS

The names of the four bad children in this story have unpleasant or ironic associations. Ask students to work out what they might be: Augustus Gloop (onomatopoeia of 'gloop', an unpleasant noise), Veruca Salt ('veruca' sounds like a name – like Veronica – but it is a type of infectious corn you get on your foot), Violet Beauregarde (has nothing like a 'beau regard'), Mike Teavea (TV).

Tell students that they will be writing a story that takes place in the factory they imagined and drew the beginning. In small groups brainstorm some good names for characters.

*Writing*

They should write the story which takes place in the factory they drew. Students can write individually or in groups. It is probably better to do the planning stage in groups. They can choose one drawing for the whole group if they write the actual story together.

*Discussion*

Some of the episodes in this story are quite cruel even if the 'victims' deserve what they get. Can students think of other stories that are cruel? (Prompt students with allusions to fairy stories.) Do the students like cruel stories? Do they do any harm? Is it the same thing as watching horror movies?

*Project work*

Organize a visit to a factory. Afterwards, back in class, make suggestions for improving working conditions in a factory.

*Notes prepared by Gillian Porter Ladousse*

## Section 3   Lower to Upper Secondary

### 1   ANIMAL FARM

*by George Orwell*

#### The story

This is the story of how the animals take over Manor Farm from Mr Jones, the owner. The author called it 'a fairy story' and it does indeed contain elements which link it with classical fairy stories: the animals who act like human beings are the most obvious feature.

The animals' revolt is caused by their neglect at the hands of Mr Jones and his men so the reader can sympathize with their need to rebel. But very soon the new regime begins to exercise its power, and there are battles among the animals for leadership. The pigs eventually become the strongest group and their enemies are eliminated. The new rules and regulations are bent to suit the leaders and, by the end, the democratic slogan 'All animals are equal' becomes 'All animals are equal. But some are more equal than others.' The pigs end up looking and behaving like the men they chased out of the farm, and the revolution has come full circle.

#### Level

Linguistically the story is not simple, but the plot and the characters carry the reader along quite rapidly. Some political awareness is necessary in the reader to enter more completely into the fable, so the book might be more appropriate for fifteen to sixteen year olds. It can be the first full-length text which students read in English.

#### The politics and the fairy story

George Orwell intended *Animal Farm* 'primarily [as] a satire on the Russian Revolution', but it clearly also has a wider application to any revolutionary situation. Since the changes in Eastern Europe which began in 1989, the history of Russia between the 1917 Revolution and the end of the Second World War, when this novel was written, has been radically re-evaluated and re-interpreted. This should add to the interest of the novel.

It should not be necessary to get involved in the overt political references in the story at first reading. These can be handled later.

## Point of entry

THE SEVEN COMMANDMENTS

1 Whatever goes upon two legs is an enemy.

2 Whatever goes upon four legs, or has wings, is a friend.

3 No animal shall wear clothes.

4 No animal shall sleep in a bed.

5 No animal shall drink alcohol.

6 No animal shall kill any other animal.

7 All animals are equal.

These slogans (*p. 15*) can be a useful point of entry into the book's ideas. What point of view do they represent? What do they tell the reader about the relationship between the animals and men? Point out that at the beginning the farm's name is Manor Farm (manor being a fair-sized English country house). It then becomes Animal Farm. The contrast Man(or)/Animal should appeal.

## Presentation and pre-reading stimuli

Have students heard of this novel and/or the author? If so, find out what they know. It will already be useful for them to start noting points in their reading diaries, especially if there is some (even a little) common background knowledge about the book.

If nothing is known, what do they expect from the title, the cover, the blurb on the back cover? And what kind of expectations does the subtitle ('A Fairy Story') create? These might actually be negative expectations of a moral fable about animals, especially if students have read – and not enjoyed – some other books with fable elements in them.

Stress at the outset that *Animal Farm* is rather different, referring to what is described on the back-cover blurb. How does this differ from any other fable story they have read? What do the words 'revolution', 'perversion' and 'tragic' add to their expectations?

Anticipate the first two paragraphs for the first encounter with both men and animals: What seems negative about Mr Jones in the first paragraph? And what is unexpected about Major's behaviour in the second paragraph? What seems likely to happen?

## Vocabulary and style

Already in the very first paragraph there is vocabulary which students will find unfamiliar: pop-holes, lantern, lurched, yard, drew, scullery and snoring.

In the second, words like stirring, fluttering, boar and barn could cause problems. It might, therefore, be useful to brainstorm some words under headings such as: farm animals (give boar as a kind of pig), farm buildings, human movements, sounds and so on. The vocabulary anticipated can be noted in students' reading diaries.

Then, while reading the complete novel, new words can be guessed in context with reference to these (and other) headings.

## Characters

Already in the first two paragraphs the characters of Mr Jones and Major are pretty well-defined. Invite students to think of adjectives to describe them. These can be kept for future reference and comparison. Later in the book such characters as Napoleon, Benjamin, Snowball, Squealer, Boxer, Mollie, Clover and Mr Whymper will deserve character notes and these observations can be kept in the reading diary.

These character notes could be made into charts including such headings as: kind of animal (in most cases) sex/age/appearance/personality/attitude to life/strengths/weaknesses/role on the farm/role in the story/any changes the character undergoes/final destiny. A chart in columns can be kept for every character, or at least for the main characters, and added to from time to time.

## Events

As the reading progresses, interest might be focused on key events in each chapter. These can be the subject of class discussion, interpretation and also perhaps for further written work or debate. Most of the questions should be handled *after* reading the chapter concerned, but teachers might like to use *one* of them as a pre-reading stimulus for the chapter.

## Chapter 1

Major's use of the vocative 'Comrades' (first used on *p. 3*, then throughout the story). What does it indicate in students' opinion? Does it have similar connotations in their own language?

● The nature of the animals' lives, and the problem of the enemy,

Man. Reference could be made to the making of a before and after chart (*see below*).

What does Major appeal to while speaking to the animals? Is this similar to any kind of human discourse students have heard or read?

- Major's prohibitions. What do they tell us about the differences between animals and men, and about Major's ideals and philosophy?
- What does the song 'The Beasts of England' make students think of? What elements of liberation can they find in it?

*Chapter 2*

How much time passes after Major's death, and before the rebellion?

- What is the influence of Moses, the tame raven?
- What finally drives the animals to take action against Mr Jones and his men? Make a list of the events of the Sunday, in the order in which they occurred.
- The animals are described as having certain abilities, like reading and writing. Add these to the character charts. What differences emerge between the characters?
- Begin a list or table which contrasts human behaviour (for example, wearing ribbons or clothes) and animal behaviour. This can be added to throughout the reading.
- What is the importance of the Seven Commandments in students' opinion? Why are they called Commandments? Does the first paragraph (*p. 16*) reveal anything about the narrator's attitude towards the writing of the Commandments? If so, what could it be? (This should help to bring out the increasing irony in the book. It will be important for the development of the story that students keep these Commandments in mind.)

*Chapter 3*

Sum up the work and the difficulties the animals encountered. Is the tone here positive or negative, optimistic or pessimistic?

- Do the Committees and Leagues (*p. 20*) remind students of any similar enterprises in real life?
- What do we learn about the animals' learning capabilities? Refer again to the character charts, especially for the differences which continue to emerge.
- How is the new maxim different from, better than, or easier than, the Seven Commandments?

- Why do the pigs begin to have special privileges? What is Squealer's role? Is he a sympathetic character?
- Prediction: how do students imagine the story might develop from this point?

## Chapter 4
What has Mr Jones been doing all the while?

- Describe the battle, and the reasons behind it, very briefly (three or four sentences).
- Why will the animals remember the Battle of the Cowshed?

## Chapter 5
What is wrong with Mollie?

- What differences emerge between Snowball and Napoleon?
- Why does the windmill cause such differences of opinion?
- What is Squealer's role now? What happens to Snowball? Why?

## Chapter 6
What notes give an impression that all is not going quite as well as it might?

- What part of the original ideals of the revolution is compromised with the involvement of Mr Whymper?
- How are the Commandments being changed? How many words have to be added, and what difference do they make to the original Commandments? (This will now become an ongoing question.)
- Do your students agree that it was Snowball who destroyed the windmill? This can lead to a discussion of motivations and further prediction of Napoleon's intentions.

## Chapter 7
The weather has been mentioned often. Before going on to this chapter, have students trace all the developments in the weather so far. What does the weather add to the atmosphere of the story, or to the animals' struggles?

- Why was it 'vitally necessary' to conceal the fact that food was in short supply? How did Napoleon do this?
- Is Snowball really at Pinchfield? Looking back to chapter 4, how would students describe the roles of Mr Pilkington and Mr Frederick? How are they portrayed differently from Mr Whymper or Mr Jones?

- How does Boxer react to Napoleon? And to Squealer's words? Have students' views of Boxer's character changed at all? And their view of Squealer?
- What does Napoleon's award to himself of the Order of 'Animal Hero, First Class' tell you about Napoleon?
- What effect do the executions have on the animals? And on the students themselves?
- Why is 'The Beasts of England' abolished? What has changed since it was first sung? What does the poet's name suggest to you about Minimus? How does his 'song' compare with 'The Beasts of England?

*Chapter 8*
How has the Sixth Commandment changed? (Refer back to chapter 6 for comparison. How many new words? What implications?)

- What is the function of: Squealer reading out production figures; the new poem by Minimus; the negotiations with Frederick and Pilkington?
- Why does the attack happen? What is the animals' reaction? How is this victory different from those in chapters 2 and 4?
- Why do students think Napoleon starts wearing a bowler hat?
- What really happens to Napoleon after the discovery of the whisky?
- How and why does the Fifth Commandment change?

*Chapter 9*
Do the readers sympathize with Boxer?
- Pick out words and phrases which show an improvement in the animals' quality of life.
- What do students think of the Spontaneous Demonstrations?
- What finally happens to Boxer? What is the reaction of the other animals? And of the readers?

*Chapter 10*
Looking back, try to trace how much time has passed since the beginning of the book. A class chart could be drawn up narrating the events over this period. How have the characters changed over the years? Who is missing now?
- Pick out words and phrases indicating: prosperity, hope, memory, change, disappointment.
- How is the 'Four legs good' maxim changed? And what does the change to the Commandments (*p. 90*) tell you about the course of the revolution?

- What is Mr Pilkington's role now?
- How has the use of the word 'Comrade' changed since the beginning of the story?
- What do students think of the final paragraph?

### Before and after

As well as the charts delineating aspects of character, students might like to keep before and after charts. These could show, for example, in three columns what the animals' lives were like before the revolution, immediately after the revolution and ten years after the revolution.

### Summary

Teachers might like to encourage a brief oral summary of each chapter as the reading is carried on. Certainly a short summary of the novel, when it is completed, will be useful. The narrative time-chart will be helpful also in this context. A summary of what happens to some of the main characters is another possibility.

### Moral

It is almost inevitable that students will want to draw the moral of the story. This is, in fact, largely a question of interpretation; so a fair amount of liberty can be given in the expression of the moral. Is Napoleon seen as a totally negative character? Do students identify with or sympathize with any of the characters (Mollie or Boxer, for example?). How much do students see the story as a political analogy, even without specific reference to the Russian Revolution?

### Narration

The narration is in the third person but an ironic narrative presence can frequently be detected. Have students find any examples of this which struck them to open up discussion on how these moments influence the reader's reactions. Do students think the author's own opinions emerge at any point?

### Extension – Language

Teachers might like to refer to Orwell's essay 'Politics and the English Language' (available in volume four of *The Collected Essays,*

*Letters and Journalism – In Front of Your Nose*, published by Penguin). In this essay, Orwell relates language and political decline. (The essay is by no means essential to class discussion but it is a useful reference and some students might like to read it if they want to go more deeply into Orwell and his views.)

This can open up a discussion on various closely related linguistic features of *Animal Farm* such as:

- the importance of persuasion (the role of Squealer, for instance)
- the place of memorable slogans in political discourse
- lying through language, as in Squealer's 'readjustment' instead of 'reduction' (*p. 75*) or the misuse of the adjective in 'Spontaneous Demonstration', or the role of Snowball as scapegoat after his disappearance
- 'double-speak', and how the reader can tell when the truth is being covered up, or a character is 'being economical with the truth', as in Squealer's speech (*p. 54*) and the animals' reaction: 'it seemed . . . that they did remember it'
- how far characters (animals or people) actually *want* to be convinced by their leaders and their spokespersons
- how leaders assert themselves through language.

Examples of all these linguistic phenomena will be found throughout the book. It should not be necessary to over-stress any single aspect of this discussion for the whole area of linguistic corruption as a reflection of political corruption is part of Orwell's field of concern in both the novel and the essay.

### Viewpoints

- Both Major and Snowball taught the animals to dream. How different were their dreams? And how did reality change these dreams?
- How many human characteristics – good and bad – can you find in the animals? Add them to the character charts.
- Imagine a conversation between Napoleon and Squealer when Napoleon is telling Squealer what to say about, for example, Snowball, or the whisky. What would Napoleon say?
- Imagine a conversation between Mr Pilkington and Mr Jones after the end of the novel. What would they say to each other?
- Imagine an illustrated (or cartoon) version of the story. What visual elements of character and of the farm would students emphasize?

- Can students imagine any present-day regime which might want to ban the book? Why might it be banned?

### Research and topical relevance

The last question in the previous section might lead to an examination of the historical references contained in the first edition of the novel. Critics have identified, for example, Major with Lenin, Napoleon with Stalin and Snowball with Trotsky in the context of the 1917 Russian Revolution and its aftermath. The introduction (*p. vii*) shows that Orwell took pains also to show the positive side of Stalin.

How much students will wish to pursue or examine this connection will depend on individual interpretation. How relevant do students think the book is to other regimes and other historical periods? Are there any events in more recent history which echo the plot of this novel? How have the changes in Eastern Europe since 1989 affected ways of reading *Animal Farm*?

### Conclusions

- Did students enjoy the book? Or is *enjoy* not the best word? What effect did it have on them?
- Would they recommend it to other readers? How would they encourage someone to read it?

*Notes prepared by John McRae*

## 2   THE HAPPY PRINCE AND OTHER STORIES

*by Oscar Wilde*

### Level

The stories in this book should be accessible to students of any age who have gone beyond the elementary stages of language learning. Full comprehension will be inhibited, however, by such factors as the literary convention (fairy-tale) in which they were written and the extensive vocabulary used. (Both these topics will be covered later.) The fairy-tale convention does, however, mean that the stories are, in themselves, very simple, easy to follow and of wide appeal.

### Synopsis

*The Happy Prince (pp. 13–24)*
A swallow on his way south for the winter stops beside a beautiful

statue of a prince who once lived in a palace. This statue is covered in gold and jewels, but there is poverty and misery all around it. At the request of the statue, the swallow picks these riches from him to give to the poor. The prince's statue becomes ugly and, as winter arrives, the swallow dies of cold and the heart of the statue breaks.

### The Selfish Giant (pp. 27–32)

A giant forbids children to play in his garden; from that time on it is permanently winter. The children come in again and spring arrives; the giant is happy. One child kisses him but is not seen again. The giant makes his garden into a children's playground. The missing child returns, bearing the stigmata of Christ. The giant dies and goes to Paradise.

### The Devoted Friend (pp. 35–48)

The story is told to a water-rat, who says friendship is greater than love. The story concerns little Hans, who is poor, and the miller, a rich man who says he is Hans's friend. The miller has never given gifts or hospitality to Hans, but promises to give him a wheelbarrow. Hans gives gifts to the miller and does many jobs at the miller's request. Hans dies in a storm on an errand for the miller. The miller still has his old wheelbarrow. When the story is finished, the water-rat complains that he is unable to appreciate its 'moral'.

### The Remarkable Rocket (pp. 51–65)

The rocket is a firework which is to be let off at the prince's wedding. He is very self-centred and critical of the other fireworks. He begins to cry (and makes himself damp) when he speculates about disaster befalling the prince and therefore cannot be part of the firework display. He is thrown away into a ditch. Various animals tell him he is useless, but he remains supercilious. Two boys put him on a fire to help boil some water; he explodes into the air. Nobody sees him, but he is unaware of this.

### The Nightingale and the Rose (pp. 69–76)

A student complains that his professor's daughter will not dance with him unless he gives her a red rose. A nightingale pities him, but no red rose is available. The nightingale presses her heart against a thorn and a red rose grows – but the bird dies. The student picks the rose and takes it to the professor's daughter but she rejects it. The student throws away the rose and returns to his studies.

(The above five stories were first published in May 1888; the subsequent four stories – generally longer and thematically more complex – were collected in the volume *A House of Pomegranates*, first published in November 1891.)

### The Young King (pp. 79–95)

The young king was raised by a peasant family, but was recognized by the old king on his death-bed as his grandson. The youth has always admired beautiful things but, the night before his coronation, the young king dreams of wretched workmen, reduced to misery to make this a splendid event. The next morning he appears in peasant dress. The bishop is perplexed but, as the young king kneels in prayer, a divine light enters the cathedral, transforming the youth's rags to splendour and leaving all onlookers awestruck.

### The Birthday of the Infanta (pp. 99–121)

On the twelfth birthday of the infanta, her father the king – now an unhappy widower – allows her to witness an entertainment given by the common people. The most amusing performer is a dancing dwarf, who seems unaware of his grotesque appearance. The infanta throws a rose to the dwarf and commands him to dance for her again the same evening; the dwarf believes she loves him. He comes to the palace to find her. Stopping in front of a mirror, he sees a deformed monster. The infanta enters just as he realizes this is his own image. She is amused at his writhing in agony on the floor and is unaware that he is dying of a broken heart.

### The Star Child (pp. 125–43)

On a cold night, a star falls to earth. Where it fell, two poor woodcutters find a baby boy. The beautiful child grows up vain and cruel. Years later, a foul old woman passes, saying she lost her child in the woods. Despite the evidence, the boy refuses to acknowledge the woman as his mother. He immediately becomes ugly and, repenting, seeks without success for the mother he now recognizes. He becomes slave to a magician, who sends him three times to find gold. Each time the boy gives away the gold to a leper. Returning the third time, he is acclaimed as a prince. Uncomprehending, he recognizes his mother and, weeping, asks for pardon. The beggar-woman is transformed into a queen and the leper becomes a king. The star child becomes a just and generous ruler.

*The Fisherman and His Soul (pp. 147–86)*

A fisherman catches a mermaid and falls in love with her. But they cannot remain together because the fisherman has a human soul. He enters into a pact with a witch and, at a night-time gathering, he is separated from his shadow – his soul. The fisherman joins his mermaid lover. The (disembodied) soul describes two journeys, offering to rejoin the fisherman's body in the name of wisdom and of riches. The soul's third description is of a dancing girl and the fisherman leaves his mermaid. Over the next few days, the fisherman has many bad thoughts and performs many bad deeds. Eventually recognizing his fault, he blames the evil soul who has accompanied him. He returns to the sea, but cannot find the mermaid. The fisherman mourns for two years. Then the mermaid's dead body is cast up on the shore. The fisherman refuses to allow the soul to re-enter his body, but, as his heart breaks, the soul returns. The grave-site of the fisherman and his love remains barren of vegetation.

## Point of entry

'In the square below,' said the Happy Prince, 'there stands a little match-girl. She has let her matches fall in the gutter, and they are all spoiled. Her father will beat her if she does not bring home some money, and she is crying. She has no shoes or stockings, and her little head is bare. Pluck out my other eye, and give it to her, and her father will not beat her.'

'I will stay with you one night longer,' said the Swallow, 'but I cannot pluck out your eye. You would be quite blind then.'

'Swallow, Swallow, little Swallow,' said the Prince, 'do as I command you.'

So he plucked out the Prince's other eye, and darted down with it. He swooped past the match-girl, and slipped the jewel into the palm of her hand. 'What a lovely bit of glass!' cried the little girl; and she ran home, laughing.

Then the Swallow came back to the Prince. 'You are blind now,' he said, 'so I will stay with you always.'

This passage from 'The Happy Prince' (*p. 20, l. 32 to p. 21, l. 14*) demonstrates many aspects of the fairy-tale convention provided it is made clear that the Prince is a statue and his eye a jewel.

The main character here is strongly motivated towards deeds of generosity which require the assistance of an active agent, in this case the swallow. Students may recognize both sentimental and moralizing elements in the passage, to orientate themselves into the story.

### Presentation and pre-reading stimuli

The convention of the fairy-tale can perhaps best be introduced by a series of questions. You may, for instance, begin by asking if students are familiar with the stories of Hans Christian Andersen, the fables of La Fontaine, or the folk tales collected by the brothers Jacob and Wilhelm Grimm. If they are, ask *when* students first encountered these authors. Was it when they were very young? Do students consider fairly-tales to be the exclusive province of very young children? How do they feel about being asked to read these stories now? What do they hope to gain from doing so?

Ask students to mention any fairy-tale elements they can recall. Some of these might be: noble characters, magic spells, fantasy worlds, simple black-and-white morality. Then ask them to explain how the world represented in the fairy-tales differed from the real-life world of today.

Is the cover of the book attractive to them? What about the picture on the title page? Do students have any initial reaction to the list of titles given on the Contents page?

To encourage a spontaneous response to the text, it is best to advise students against reading the publisher's blurb or Mac Liammóir's Introduction before they have read the fairy-tales themselves.

### Reading

This reading can be organized in two stages and should take place outside the classroom. For the first stage have all students read *one* of the stories. In Follow-up activities A, ideas are suggested for handling a class discussion of the first story, 'The Happy Prince', after *all* students have read this text.

For the second stage, have students choose and read one of the remaining eight stories in groups of no less than two and no more than five (assuming classes do not exceed forty students). This will enable students to compare their differing reactions to the same text. Then there can be further activities, for which guidelines are suggested in Follow-up activities B.

Students may then progress to a full reading of the book. A final (very much optional) extension to their reading is given in Follow-up activities C.

## Vocabulary

In general this should not be a problem, but there are some 'purple passages' which might slow down the reading. Some examples may be: 'The Happy Prince' (*p. 21, the paragraph beginning 'All the next day . . .'*); 'The Nightingale and the Rose' (*bottom of p. 71 to end of first paragraph, p. 72*); 'The Young King' (*pp. 81–3*).

Some explanation, preferably *after* an initial reading, will be necessary. It is essential to impress upon students that it is not necessary to know the literal meaning of every single word in the text (many native speakers of English will not know all the words Wilde used).

To give an example, the following passage comes from 'The Birthday of the Infanta' (*p. 118*):

> The walls were covered with a pink-flowered Lucca damask, patterned with birds and dotted with dainty blossoms of silver; the furniture was of massive silver, festooned with florid wreaths, and swinging Cupids; in front of the two large fire-places stood great screens broidered with parrots and peacocks, and the floor, which was of sea-green onyx, seemed to stretch far away into the distance.

The essential thing here is to recognize that Wilde is describing a fabulous room in a royal palace. It does not matter if students cannot say what 'Lucca damask' or 'sea-green onyx' mean; even the adjectives 'massive' and 'florid' and the verbs 'festooned' and 'broidered' should not deter the receptive reader from an appreciation of the Dwarf's wonderment when he enters the Infanta's private room.

## Illustrations

Students' responses to the text may be guided by the pictures to reinforce or to negate their reactions. Ask whether they like them or not. Do the illustrations reflect the images which students themselves visualize?

It is important to note that the illustrations were added much later, when the stories were republished, and represent the impressions of one single reader, an artist, from many millions who have read the stories in the past hundred years or more. (The same argument might be applied to Mac Liammóir's Introduction.)

## Moral

See if students can identify the moral of each story. In most cases these will be quite obvious, although (unlike La Fontaine, for example) they remain implicit in the text rather than stated as a postscript. After examining the moral(s), this quotation might be used to stimulate discussion: 'There is no such thing as a moral or an immoral book. Books are well written, or badly written. That is all.' (Oscar Wilde from the Preface to *The Picture of Dorian Gray*.)

The doctrine of Christianity underlies many of the stories; readers of 'The Selfish Giant', for example, should recognize the Christ-child (*p. 32*) when he returns to consign the guilty hero to Paradise. The final story, 'The Fisherman and his Soul', would similarly lose some of its impact if students did not recognize that Christianity teaches people to value the inner life ('the soul') above the external life of human interaction.

Other stories demonstrate Wilde's socialist sympathies. 'The Happy Prince' and 'The Young King', for example, both invite readers to identify with the dilemma of a privileged person who not only feels sorry for the poverty and misery of his fellow men and women but wishes to take positive action to overcome it.

## Reading diary

For work done outside the classroom, it is always advisable to ask students to keep a diary of the reading tasks they are fulfilling, with notes on their reactions, on any vocabulary items (or longer quotations) they want to remember, and on elements which can be used to compare and contrast the stories. Notes should be detailed enough subsequently to be built up into either oral or written summaries.

## Follow-up activities

### A *The Happy Prince*

The reading of one story by all members of the class will help to reinforce many observations which may be applied to all the stories in the book. This story is typical of others in the volume; above all it will give students some idea of the language they will have to deal with in their further reading.

When discussing the story, ask for passages students liked very much, liked but did not fully understand, did not like at all (ask students to say why or why not). Some assistance at this stage with problematic linguistic features will probably make students' further reading tasks much easier.

Various themes will emerge. Discussion could usefully be focused on one or more of the following: the Prince's feeling of guilt; the anthropomorphic elements; the swallow's motivation for remaining with the Prince.

More serious discussion might take up the idea that personal happiness can be derived only from giving happiness to other people. There is usually an 'agent' – in this case, the swallow – who turns thoughts into deeds. And finally, there is often a pay-off; that is to say, there is some kind of change at the end of the story. In this case, good deeds are rewarded by the approval of God.

In most stories, there is an obvious change of circumstances between the beginning and the end, which helps to draw attention to the 'moral': for example, the Selfish Giant admits the children to his garden; the Fisherman rejects the Soul, which has encouraged his bad deeds. In the case of the Happy Prince, his heart breaks after the death of the swallow, but the 'moral' is that he has completed his good work, using the swallow as his agent. How do students react to the comments of the Councillors (*p. 23*)?

## B *Other stories*
After reading – in groups of two to five, outside the classroom – students who have read the same story should be invited to get together and discuss their reactions. The teacher must follow at least some of the discussion which arises. Dissent between group members is quite likely and should not be discouraged.

One or more members of each of the eight groups should then be invited to give an oral summary to the class. From those students who do not have the opportunity to speak to the class, a development of their notes into a written summary may be requested.

Following each *oral* summary, time should be allowed for questions and comments from other members of the class who have *not* read the story being summarized. Similarities and differences between the story they have heard about and the story they have themselves read should motivate students to compare and contrast, to find out common themes for themselves.

At this stage, students can proceed to a reading of all the stories. They may even feel encouraged to do so voluntarily!

## C Dramatization

The stories themselves are full of drama and perhaps students would like to dramatize some of them. For example, 'The Happy Prince' would require only two 'actors' – the Prince and the swallow – plus a narrator. Most of the other stories are equally simple in dramatic terms.

Students will want to take their reading further; and dramatization is a relevant and enjoyable step forward from the study of these stories.

*Notes prepared by Jeremy Hunter*

# 3   CALL OF THE WILD

### *by Jack London*

**The story**

This is an adventure story with a hero, a dog called Buck. His parents were a St Bernard and a Scottish sheepdog. Buck is four years old in 1897 when he is taken away and sold to a man who wields a club. So begin Buck's adventures which are told from the dog's point of view, although the story is narrated in the third person. We feel and suffer with Buck as he is badly treated on the way to the Gold Fields of the Klondike. Here the men need good strong dogs to help them with their work, especially to pull heavy loads on sledges over the expanses of the frozen wastes.

There is 'no law but the law of the club and fang' in the Klondike: the clubs of the masters, who very often treat their animals badly; the fangs or teeth of the other dogs – the wolf-dogs – who, like the men, are savages. Buck suffers, but survives, and the reader shares his suffering and his triumphs as he becomes leader of all the dogs of the Klondike: a living legend. The story of his relationship with John Thornton, his good new master is deeply moving and very exciting, as man and dog face the challenges of the most difficult climate and landscape in the world.

**Point of entry**

John Thornton stood over Buck, struggling to control himself, too convulsed with rage to speak.

'If you strike that dog again, I'll kill you,' he at last managed to say in a choking voice.

'It's my dog,' Hal replied, wiping the blood from his mouth as
he came back. 'Get out of my way, or I'll fix you. I'm going to
Dawson.'

Thornton stood between him and Buck, and evinced no
intention of getting out of the way.

The relationship between Buck, the dog, and John Thornton
emerges clearly if this passage (*p. 83, ll. 13–22*) is used as point of
entry. Why do students think John Thornton so strongly wants to
defend the dog? Who might want to strike a dog? What kind of
person does Hal seem to be?

The passage will also serve to show that *Call of the Wild* is more
than 'just' an animal story for the sense of danger and adventure
comes across immediately.

### Presentation and pre-reading stimuli

Ask students what the title brings to mind. Suggestions might
include the Wild West, the depths of the jungle and so on. What
will emerge are two key aspects: unexplored territory and a sense
of adventure; and nature in a threatening rather than in a peaceful
sense.

Move on to the idea of the Gold Rush. Where did it happen and
when? If possible refer to maps to pinpoint California and the
Klondike in Western Canada. This is where the story is set as Buck
is kidnapped from a comfortable home in California – a state
already rich from earlier gold rushes – and taken to the snowy
wastes of the Klondike and the Yukon, as far north as what is now
Alaska. (Keep a map available to trace Buck's journeys during the
reading.)

What will life be like in the Klondike? Why then do people go
there? Ask students what they would be prepared to do if they
thought they could find gold. Would they give up their homes and
families, suffer deprivation, cold and hunger and fight?

Elicit their attitudes to animals. Are students fond of them?
Should animals be used in the service of mankind? Remind them
of the saying 'a dog is a man's best friend'. Do they agree? Have
them tell their own experiences with animals, especially stories of
loyalty and courage. Then move on to any stories they may know,
or have heard, about the harsh treatment of animals.

Ask what they feel about animal stories. Some students may
react negatively, thinking of the ultra-sweet *Lassie* or *Black Beauty*
as typical animal stories. Have them say why they do or don't like
them. Anthropomorphism (animals reacting, thinking and speaking as if they were human) is at the heart of the question, but

what will emerge is more likely to be that readers prefer animals to be animals and humans humans. Students are likely to consider childish the idea of animals speaking, or of writers trying to make animals too human. Reassurance might be needed that Jack London' s approach is quite different.

To enter into the atmosphere and spirit of the story some teachers might like to give a brief outline of London's own career and experiences in the Klondike, as these are very much the basis of his adventure stories. Other teachers will want to keep this kind of background information until after the reading, perhaps making a research project or information-gathering exercise out of it.

### Background

Jack London (1876–1916) was born in poverty, and his writings take two distinct lines as a result: social novels about poverty and slum life, and adventure novels of the Gold Rush and the harsh life of people prepared to risk everything for the dream of great wealth.

London himself took part in the Klondike Gold Rush of 1897, so *Call of the Wild* is based on his own experience. The violence, the privation and suffering, the details of the adventurers' lives are all realistic, so there is no risk of the romantic animal tale. What sets London apart is his concern for man's inhumanity towards other men, and towards the animals which were such an essential part of their lives in the Klondike.

### Reading strategies

Students should be encouraged, while reading the story, to look out for some of the characteristic concerns of London's writing: violent behaviour – can it ever be justified?; learning to be strong in adversity; trust and misplaced trust; the survival of the fittest; injustice and overcoming it. Notes can be made in a reading diary, detailing where students have found these themes.

At the beginning of the story, the rather wordy style, with long sentences, may cause a little resistance. Use the promise of 'unmiss-able scenes' to encourage reading on. For the first page, the following questions can be used: why does Buck not read news-papers?; what would he read in them anyway?; what is the yellow metal?; what are the results of finding this metal?; why is this a danger to dogs?; what kind of life does Buck lead now? This can lead to predictions as to what is going to happen to Buck. Use the cover illustration to stimulate ideas.

The book should be read chapter by chapter, and, if possible, students should read the complete chapter before discussing it in class. The chapter titles should encourage ideas of what might happen. These predictions should be noted down and then compared with what actually does happen in the class discussion afterwards.

### Illustrations

The illustrations (*pp. 7, 17, 28, 56–7, 70–71, 93, 100 and 123*) can be used before reading by students to identify what might be happening. Or, after the reading, students should be able to point out the exact textual references of the illustrations. Then they can comment on how effective (or not) a particular illustration is.

Discussion might arise as to how much the illustrations resemble Buck as the students imagine him (he looks more like an Alsatian or German Shepherd than a mix of St Bernard and Scottish sheepdog!). Students with an artistic bent might like to attempt other illustrations of attractive scenes in the chapters already read.

### Vocabulary

Anticipate or brainstorm vocabulary to do with snow, sledges, harnesses, etc. Collect negative words for scenes of suffering (*pp. 78–9*, for example) and words for strength, endurance and dogs (fangs, coat, paws). Building up these vocabulary areas in students' reading diaries means that when they find unfamiliar words they can put them under the above headings, guess at their meaning, and check on them in class, without constantly having to stop and look them up in the dictionary.

Point out that there are some dialect forms (*p. 18*, for example) representing, naturally enough, the speech patterns of the adventurers ('ain't' he isn't; 'druther' I'd rather).

### During reading

The following guidelines attempt to select some of the most 'unmissable' moments of the story, and give the very brief summary that students should aim at in summing up 'the story so far' at the beginning of every class discussion of their ongoing reading.

*p. 10, l. 8–p. 19, l. 11:* Buck is stolen, maltreated and learns a new lesson.

*p. 21, l. 29–p. 22:* Buck's initiation to snow.

*pp. 23–5, l. 19:* Buck's first experience of dogs fighting, and of the harness.

*p. 30, l. 18–p. 32, l. 31:* Buck becomes a working dog on the trail.

*p. 33, l. 20–p. 34:* The return of old, basic dog instincts.

*p. 41, l. 8–p. 43, l. 28:* Buck defends himself against a mad dog, Dolly, and against his enemy, Spitz.

*p. 47, l. 21–p. 52:* The challenge between Buck and Spitz.

*p. 55, l. 25–p. 57:* Buck as the natural leader.

*p. 58, l. 31–p. 64:* Work, Buck's memories and the end of the trail for Dave.

*p. 65–p. 67, l. 23:* Changes: new owners. Will they be good or bad?

*p. 72, l. 18–p. 75, l. 31:* Negative experiences with the new owners.

*p. 78, l. 10–p. 79, l. 19:* The dogs' suffering.

*p. 81. l. 4–p. 84:* Arrival at John Thornton's camp.

*p. 85–p. 92, l. 10:* Buck's reputation grows through his love for John Thornton.

*p. 95, l. 26–p. 102:* The challenge, for money, to Buck's strength.

*p. 104, l. 6–p. 113, l. 2:* The Triumph: 'never was there such a dog'. What conclusion do students predict to the story?

*p. 117, l. 10–p. 121, l. 3:* The Yeehat Indians attack, Buck's revenge, the death of John Thornton.

*p. 123, l. 1–p. 124:* Buck joins the wolves and the legend begins. (This omits one or two very famous passages. Buck's rescue of John Thornton is perhaps the best known of them (*pp. 92–5*).)

### Adventure story or moral fable?

Because the story is seen through Buck's eyes, an element of judgement is often present. How do students judge: the kidnapper, the various owners, Spitz, the shooting of Dave, John Thornton, Matthewson's bet, the final scene?

Do students feel there is a 'message' that the author wants to put across? What might it be?

### What if?

A useful game to exercise students' imagination, with a little grammar too. It can be written or oral work, possibly in pairs or groups, on questions like:

● What if Buck's Californian owners had kept him in a kennel?
● What if Spitz had been a little more intelligent?
● What if Buck hadn't been a good working dog?
● What if he hadn't met John Thornton?

● What if the Indians hadn't attacked?

Many more similar questions might come from the students themselves.

### True or false
True or false questions can be used at any stage of the reading. Students can make up their own after the teacher has suggested one or two. Then go rapidly round the class:
● Buck is a St Bernard.
● Dave is the same kind of dog as Buck.
● The bet was for $1,000.
● The Indian tribe was the Watchees.
● Buck was born in San Francisco, and so on.

Answers should always be given in full. For example, 'No, he wasn't. He was born in Santa Clara Valley.' If students don't know the answer, they should find it in the text.

### Final reactions
Oral and/or written work summing-up: what readers have got out of the book; what they have learned about worlds they did not know, how they feel about the style and the kind of book it is, whether they would recommend the book to others.

Every expression of opinion should be justified, backed up from the text, if possible, and objectively reasoned. During the reading, students are subjectively involved: now is the time for more objectively considered reactions and responses.

*Notes prepared by John McRae*

## 4   TREASURE ISLAND

*by Robert Louis Stevenson*

### The story
This is Jim Hawkins's story. He tells, in the first person (with the exception of *chapters 16 to 18*), the story of his adventures with pirates in the search for treasure buried on Treasure Island, involving the classic characters Long John Silver, Squire Trelawney, Blind Pew, Ben Gunn, and the parrot, Captain Flint, who always cries 'Pieces of Eight'.

The story opens at the 'Admiral Benbow', an inn owned by Jim's father (who dies at *p. 17*). An old sailor ('an old sea dog') sings the famous song which is like an anthem throughout the book, 'Fifteen men on a dead man's chest'. He is old Billy Bones and in his chest, or trunk, there is a secret which many people would like to find. The first person to try is Black Dog – and the old sailor sends him running (*chapter 2*). Then the atmosphere of mystery deepens as a blind man arrives. The sound of his stick 'tap-tapping' in the distance is one of the most chilling and memorable effects in the book (*p. 26*) and he brings 'the black spot', the sign of death. Soon afterwards, old Billy Bones dies: the black spot has had its effect. In the old sailor's chest Jim finds a map (*pp. 38–9*) and it shows where the treasure of Captain Flint, the most famous and feared of all pirates, is buried.

Jim goes to sea in the *Hispaniola* with Squire Trelawney and Doctor Livesey. Now we meet Long John Silver, the one-legged pirate, who is the most vivid character in the story (*p. 48*). He and his cronies plot to kill the Squire and take the map, but Jim overhears their plan from his hiding-place in the apple-barrel (*chapter 11*).

Once they reach the island, the search for the treasure begins with Long John Silver trying all the time to beat Jim to it. They find an old man on the island, Ben Gunn, abandoned there by pirates (*chapter 15*). He helps Jim and the two sides battle it out (*chapter 18*) in an exciting series of attacks (*chapter 21*) until the climax 'in the enemy's camp' (*chapter 28*). But just when the treasure hunt reaches its end, the treasure is found to be gone! (*chapter 32*).

This provokes Long John Silver's crew to violence. Jim meets up with the Squire again. Of course, the treasure is finally found safe and sound. Long John Silver escapes, taking a little for himself (*p. 223*), and the rest return home in triumph with the treasure.

### Level

This is an easy story to read, full of action and excitement. Readers of thirteen and up who have studied English for three or four years will be able to read it with enjoyment.

### Vocabulary, language and style

Some evocative nautical and piratical terms create the atmosphere, so it will help to brainstorm or anticipate words like: sea dog, chest, buccaneer, crew, tar, grog (alcoholic drink), pieces of eight (gold coins), capstan (a device for hauling in ship's ropes), pigtail, anchor, mast, sails, cutlass, weather-eye (used to mean 'attention'), deck, stern, keel, shipshape, swashbuckling (meaning exciting, adventurous). This kind of vocabulary throughout need create no difficulties. If students keep a reading diary they can note down unfamiliar words under the headings where they think the meaning lies: sea and ships, food and drink/weapons/sailors' talk, piracy, other.

Spoken language is frequently rendered as it would sound when the sailors use it: 'axing' for asking, 'sityated' for situated, 'mought' for might/ought, and so on. Encourage students to work back from the *sound* to a close, recognizably familiar word, and to point out the correct spelling!

### Point of entry

When we were about half way through, I suddenly put my hand upon her arm; for I had heard in the silent, frosty air, a sound that brought my heart into my mouth – the tap-tapping of the blind man's stick upon the frozen road. It drew nearer and nearer, while we sat holding our breath. Then it struck sharp on the inn door, and then we could hear the handle being turned, and the bolt rattling as the wretched being tried to enter; and then there was a long time of silence both within and without. At last the tapping recommenced, and, to our indescribable joy and gratitude, died slowly away again until it ceased to be heard.

The famous sound of the tap-tap of Blind Pew's stick coming towards the inn (*p. 26 second last paragraph*) can be an unforgettable introduction to the story, especially if the passage is read aloud to bring out the full horror felt by Jim, the narrator.

The recent film, starring Charlton Heston as Long John Silver, can also be related to the reading of the story, and can be compared with students' expectations regarding character, setting, pace and effects such as the tap-tap of the blind man's stick.

### Presentation and pre-reading stimuli

Use the front cover for initial stimulus. Ask students to identify what is happening. Who is holding the gun? How can they tell he is a pirate? How can they tell the setting is an island? What do they think the young man being attacked has done to incur the wrath of the pirate? (Point out the empty chest, if necessary.)

Move on to what students know about pirates and pirates' tales.

What do these stories have in common? (Treasure, violence, excitement, etc.) Ask students to list the traditional elements they would expect, so that they can check them off during their reading.

Have students describe the characters on the cover, especially the attacker (notice the hat and the wooden leg), before introducing him as Long John Silver and his victim as Jim Hawkins. How can they tell which is likely to be the hero, which the villain? Is a pirate necessarily a villain? Why or why not?

This story, the classic of pirate stories, encapsulates the tradition completely: the lad Jim, the parrot, the one-legged villain (who is initially quite attractive), the squire, the map, the abandoned old pirate, the mutinous crew, the old sailor who dies, tales of revenge and bad blood, and so on, with a few features invented by Stevenson to raise his story above the ordinary.

### Prediction and summary

Do students expect a realistic story? Why or why not? Collect adjectives which they think might describe the story (romantic, realistic, exaggerated, true, etc.). These can be confirmed or refuted during the reading.

Use the chapter headings in the Contents section (*p. v*), both before and during the reading, for prediction. What do students think will happen? These chapter headings will also be a useful starting-point for a brief oral summary of five or six sentences. If these are contributed by five or six different students, the whole class can then become involved in what has been left out, what has been included, etc. (*See also the next section.*)

### Reading strategies

The chapters are of a fairly regular and approachable length, so encourage quite rapid chapter-by-chapter reading. This is a story where nothing should be skipped as each chapter contributes significantly to the overall development of the plot: 'What's going to happen next?' will always be the most pressing question. But in class time do elicit all the plot elements as they come up, using future reference, for example, 'What do you think the map is going to mean for Jim?', 'What do you think Jim will do now after overhearing the crew's conspiracy?' (*after chapter 11*). Similarly check that students realize why the narrative passes to Doctor Livesey for three chapters. What is happening to Jim in the meantime?

*Facts around the class*

A quick way to elicit an oral summary is for one student to give a fact (for example, Jim Hawkins lives at the 'Admiral Benbow Inn'), and the next student has to follow on with a related fact (for example, an old sea dog comes to the inn). This can be done rapidly or in detail, involving as many of the class as possible. If someone gives a mistaken fact, the others should be listening in order to contradict it.

### Geography

The dedication and the lines 'to the hesitating purchaser' can happily be ignored, but the map (*opposite p. 1*) can be very useful. Have students look for any names they may recognize. Are the places real? Is the island, therefore, likely to be real? This can lead on to a discussion of whether the idea of buried treasure is only a fantasy, or whether there can be some truth in the idea. Did pirates actually bury their treasure and keep maps of where it was buried?

Where is this particular treasure island in modern terms? Students, while reading, should keep an eye open for geographical references to see how many, both in England and at sea, are genuine.

When the narrative reaches the island, have students draw a map of the geographical features as they are mentioned. They should then compare their maps with the one given at the beginning of the novel.

### What if?

The game to exercise students' imagination, with some grammar work as well.

- What if Captain Bones hadn't come to the 'Admiral Benbow'?
- What if Jim hadn't found the map?
- What if Jim's father had lived?
- What if Captain Flint had not drawn up the map?
- What if Squire Trelawney and Doctor Livesey hadn't gone with Jim?
- What if the *Hispaniola* had had a different cook?
- What if Long John Silver had the use of both his legs?
- What if Long John Silver's parrot had died?
- What if Ben Gunn had been able to escape from the island?
- What if there was no treasure after all?, and so on.

## *True or false?*

This game is a good aid to comprehension and it can be tied in with the oral summary. For example:

● Jim Hawkins is twenty-two years old.
● Jim's father goes with him to the island.
● The ship is called the *Victory*.
● The treasure belonged originally to Captain Flint.
● The parrot used to belong to Captain Flint.
● Long John Silver is basically a good man.
● Doctor Livesey is Jim's enemy.
● Ben Gunn used to be a pirate, and so on.

Answers should always be given in full. For example, 'No he wasn't. He was . . .'

## *Character, motive and point of view*

Because there is such a rich gallery of characters it may be worth exploring them from various points of view, either in class discussion or in post-reading oral and written work. This gives students the possibility to enter into the minds of the characters, and see the narration from their individual viewpoints.

For example, the following questions could be raised:

● Did Bones want Jim to go looking for the treasure? Give his thoughts on the matter.
● Set up a role-play interviewing Blind Pew about why he brought the black spot.
● Write down Jim's father's last thoughts and his dying words.
● Interview Long John Silver for the job of cook on the *Hispaniola*. The Squire might be one of the interviewers.
● Make up the crew's conversation in chapter 11.
● Imagine Jim's mother's thoughts while he is away. (Perhaps as she might discuss them with a neighbour or with customers at the inn.)
● Keep Ben Gunn's diary of life on the island.
● Write an article entitled 'Why I went to Treasure Island' by Long John Silver.
● Tell of Jim's recounting of his impressions of Long John Silver to his grandchildren.
● What were Ben Gunn's feelings on returning to civilization?
● Compile a police report on Jim Hawkins's new-found wealth.
● Why did they go to Treasure Island at all? They could have stayed at home! Discuss.

## Challenges ('devil's advocate')

Invite students to take up positions which are the opposite of what they really think or feel, then defend them against challenges by the rest of the class. This can be done in groups, or with one student against the others. Possible positions:

- The treasure is just a capitalist myth.
- Pirates were right to try to steal as much treasure as they could.
- Jim Hawkins is a wet.
- Long John Silver is the hero of the story.
- Long John Silver is the devil personified.
- Sailors drink too much.
- Ben Gunn was happier on the island than he will be back in England.
- The Squire is a representative of an oppressive class.
- *Treasure Island* is just a silly story for children.

## Final reactions

Oral and/or written work summing-up: what readers have got out of the book, whether they enjoyed it, whether they would have preferred there to be a deeper moral to the story, how they feel about the style and the kind of book it is, whether they would recommend the book to others.

Every expression of opinion should be justified, backed up from the text if possible, and objectively reasoned. During the reading, students are carried along by the excitement of the story: now is the time for more objectively considered reactions and responses.

*Notes prepared by John McRae*

# 5   COLLECTED SHORT STORIES Volume 1

### *by W. Somerset Maugham*

## The stories

Often there is little action in Somerset Maugham's stories, for they are mostly to do with characters and their psychology, and with moral stances on such issues as class, race, money and so-called 'civilized' society. The writer criticizes and satirizes the fashionable views of his time with a great deal of irony, which may not be immediately obvious to students. Some of the stories also display strong and genuine emotion. There is often a sudden twist towards the end of the stories, which students should be encouraged to look out for.

### Vocabulary

Short stories are a way of introducing students to extensive reading in English, and of training them to read without necessarily understanding every single word. This objective needs to be clearly stated to prevent them from being discouraged and to wean them from the habit of reaching for the dictionary every time they do not understand a word. Of course, dictionaries should not be banned totally, but they should be used with moderation (*see the Introduction on p. 10*). For this reason, do not provide lengthy vocabulary notes. However, if you think there are some key words which will prevent your students getting the point of a story, you can provide essential vocabulary items for them on a separate sheet or on the board.

### Level

The very short stories are suitable for students of fourteen plus. The others would be appropriate for more advanced learners.

### Point of entry

I caught sight of her at the play and in answer to her beckoning I went over during the interval and sat down beside her. It was long since I had last seen her and if someone had not mentioned her name I hardly think I would have recognized her. She addressed me brightly.

'Well, it's many years since we first met. How time does fly! We're none of us getting any younger. Do you remember the first time I saw you? You asked me to luncheon.'

Did I remember?

It is a dangerous thing to order the lives of others and I have often wondered at the self-confidence of politicians, reformers and suchlike who are prepared to force upon their fellows measures that must alter their manners, habits and points of view. I have always hesitated to give advice, for how can one advise another how to act unless one knows that other as well as one knows oneself? Heaven knows, I know little enough of myself: I know nothing of others.

The beginnings of two of the very shortest stories offer suitable points of entry to both the style and the content of the volume. The first nine lines of 'The Luncheon' (*p. 97*) show nicely how Maugham sets up a situation and then creates a sense of expectancy in the reader.

Similarly, the first eight lines of 'The Happy Man' (*p. 323*) give an immediate impression of the narrator and arouse the reader's curiosity as to how the subject of interference in the lives of others will be developed.

There have been several film and other versions of these stories ('Rain' has been filmed several times, for example, and Jeffrey Archer has written a variant on 'The Luncheon'). These can be useful reference points before or during the reading of the stories.

### Reading
Generally speaking, a) exercises are pre-reading activities. These set up a frame of reference for the story, often by relating the theme to the students' own lives. They may also be predicting exercises. b) and c) are comprehension or extension exercises which are to be done while reading or after reading the story. At the end of the Notes on individual stories, you will find a short selection of general, short-story exercises.

### I Very Short Stories
There are several very short stories of between four and six pages in this collection, and it is probably easier for students to begin with these.

#### THE LUNCHEON
A young writer is flattered and then taken for a ride by an older woman.

a) Ask students to imagine they were being taken out to dinner by a favourite relative and that they can eat whatever they like on the menu. Money is no object. Ask them to list and compare what they would like.

b) Stop students reading before they get to the last short paragraph. Ask them to predict how the young man got his revenge.

c) Why did the young man take the woman out to lunch in the first place? Do you have any sympathy for him?

THE ANT AND THE GRASSHOPPER

This is a modern reversal of La Fontaine's fable.

a) The class might remember the fable as a class story. If so, a re-telling is possible: one student begins with one sentence, the next one adds a sentence and so on till the whole story is told. Alternatively, ask students to remember and relate the story in small groups.

b) After reading the story, ask students to discuss in pairs which of the characters, the ant or the grasshopper, was really the wiser. Can they think of situations in which it would be better to be the grasshopper? The pairs report back to the whole class.

HOME

This is a moving story of an old man returning home to die.

a) Discussion in pairs or as a whole class about what 'home' is.
   ● Is it where you were born?
   ● Is it where you live now?
   ● Is it where your parents or grandparents live or lived?
   ● Is it anywhere in the country you live now or were born in?

b) If it is not too sensitive a topic, you can ask students to discuss where they would like to finish their days, and why. Or you can ask what would be an 'ideal' home.

THE ESCAPE

A man gets out of a promise of marriage in a clever way.

a) Write the title of the story on the board. Ask students in pairs or groups of three to imagine a story called 'The Escape'. Each group recounts the theme of their story to the whole class. Alternatively, students can write a story for homework individually or in pairs and you can stick the stories to the wall (or photocopy a class set) so that everybody can read them.

b) A morality scale: What do you think of the characters? Consider Roger and Ruth's behaviour and rate them on the following five-point scale, giving your reasons: good, better than average, normal, worse than average, bad.

_____    _____    _____    _____    _____

c) Which character do you prefer? Give reasons.

THE JUDGEMENT SEAT

A charming, subversive and heavily ironical tale about what may happen on the day of judgement. It might lend itself to cross-curriculum exploitation with the philosophy or religious studies teacher.

MR KNOW-ALL

A know-all accepts to look a fool to save a woman's honour.

a) Check that students know the meaning of the title. Ask them in pairs or small groups to talk about any know-alls they have known and what they feel about them.

b) Why does Kelada change his mind about the pearls? Were the pearls real or not? How do you think Mrs Ramsay acquired them?

c) What does this story tell you about English attitudes to foreigners – at least at the time Somerset Maugham was writing?

THE HAPPY MAN

a) The class brainstorms their criteria for happiness (in pairs, small groups or as a whole class).

b) Compare and contrast the values the man lives by in Spain and the values he lived by in England. How has he changed? Which values do you appreciate most?

THE POET

A brief satirical comment on expectations, reality and stereotypes.

a) Ask students to describe and compare their stereotypes of poets.

b) What is the moral of this story?

c) Is this piece really a story? What are the minimum ingredients for a story?

LOUISE

A story of a 'delicate' woman who hides her real strength from everybody except the narrator.

a) Write on the board the following sentence: 'People are not always what they seem to be.' Ask students in small groups to reformulate this cliché, or to think of people it might apply to.

For example, they might come up with a sentence such as 'Some people manage to hide their real natures' or they might think of a fictional character such as Dr Jekyll and Mr Hyde.

b) Was the narrator right or wrong to tell Louise what he thought? Would you do the same thing in the same situation?

c) Do you know any characters like Louise, who appear to be very generous or selfless, but who are in fact very self-centred? Describe the ways they behave.

THE PROMISE

An older woman gives up her young husband when he falls in love with a woman of his own age.

a) Elicit the class's opinion on the question of marriage partners who are not the same age. Can you have a permanent relationship with someone who is much older or younger than you are? Is it the same for women as for men? Can happy and lasting marriages only take place between people of the same age?

b) Elizabeth Vermont is a good character to discuss on a morality scale (*see 'The Escape'*).

A STRING OF BEADS

A governess receives an unexpected windfall which enables her to live a happier, if less moral, life.

A story to compare either with 'The Fall of Edward Barnard' and 'The Happy Man' on the theme of happiness and life-styles, or with 'Mr Know-All' on the theme of jewellery, its value and its uses.

## II Tropical Stories

Somerset Maugham often uses tropical settings to bring out the contrast between the values of the civilization that he was brought up in and those of other places which can be more risky but may also be truer.

RAIN

A missionary tries to save a young woman but loses himself in the process.

a) Predicting exercise on the title. What kind of symbol could rain be? Where might the story take place?

b) Is Mr Davidson, the missionary, really 'Christian', a good man, or not? Ask students to make two columns in their notebooks, a plus column and a minus column. While they read the story, they should note 'good' actions or opinions and 'bad' actions or opinions in the appropriate column. Emphasize that you want them to note their own personal opinions. Then ask students to compare their notes and reach some conclusion about the moral worth of the character.

c) Ask students to put into their own words first what Dr Macphail 'understood' at the end of the story and then why Mr Davidson committed suicide.

Compare characters on a morality scale (*see 'The Escape'*).

THE FALL OF EDWARD BARNARD
A young man finds happiness by giving up the competitive life-style he has been brought up in.

a) It is important for readers to understand the irony of the title. To help them, predict what kind of story a 'fall' story might be: what could the character have done in order to have fallen from grace?

b) As students read the story, get them to work out the values that are discussed in the book by asking them to list those of the characters in the columns below:

| Isabel | Bateman Hunter | Edward Barnard |
|---|---|---|
| *courage* | *courage* | *freedom* |

Here are some values that may belong to one or other of the characters: honesty, happiness, wealth, fear of ridicule, caring about the opinion of others, love of money, love of nature, love of culture, sense of honour, the puritan ethic (hard work), truth, courage, beauty, freedom, goodness, spiritual life. You can put them on the board to help students fill in the grid, but do encourage them to add values of their own. Some of the values may belong in more than one column. An example is done as an illustration.

*Possible answers for the grid:*

| Isabel | Bateman Hunter | Edward Barnard |
|---|---|---|
| honesty | material wealth | happiness |
| happiness (in love and material wealth) | fear of ridicule | love of nature |
| | caring about the opinion of others | love of culture (reading) |
| truth | love of money | truth |
| love of culture (music, furniture etc.) | sense of honour | beauty |
| | courage | freedom |
| courage | puritan ethic | goodness |
| goodness | | |

c) A morality scale (*see 'The Escape'*): Which character do you prefer? Why? Which character do you think the writer feels the most sympathy with? Which life-style would you prefer?

HONOLULU

This is a story within a story within a story and takes a while to get into. It is about passion and crime and has the habitual Somerset Maugham twist at the end. It is probably more suitable for individual than classroom reading. However, you can ask students which of the following morals best fits the story?

i) You cannot expect people to be faithful.
ii) You do not have to be attractive for people to fall in love with you.
iii) People always get their just deserts.

THE POOL

This is a story of an impossible love.

a) Introduce the story with the theme of mixed marriages. Can they work? Under what circumstances? If this is too sensitive a topic, predict the theme of the story through the title.

b) On the board, list the characteristics of a tropical island culture and that of a 'civilized' culture. (For example, the natural beauty of the island and entertainment, such as the opera in Britain.) Which characteristics are most important for Lawson? And for Ethel?

c) List the attractions and the disadvantages of an island culture and a city culture for yourself. Compare your notes with a partner.

MACKINTOSH

A dramatic story about two incompatible colleagues.

a) Introduce the theme with a discussion of colonization and decolonization. What do students know? Dates? Status of different ex-colonies? Living conditions before and after colonization?

b) Put this list of adjectives which can describe character on the board: sensual, tidy, vulgar, sensitive, well-educated, hearty, fastidious, warm, sentimental, cunning, determined, resentful, hard-hearted, unattractive, shrewd. As students read the first pages of the story, ask them to write beside each adjective **W** if they think it describes Walker and **M** if they think it describes Mackintosh. They compare notes with a partner and then with the whole class.

Stop reading the story on p. 172: 'I don't want your job. You'll get all right.' Predict the ending: Will Walker get better? Will Mackintosh get his job? Will Mackintosh be accused of the murder?

c) How should Mackintosh have behaved? Was he right to kill himself?

*Discussion:* What is it that makes people friends or enemies?

BEFORE THE PARTY

A cleverly constructed story about marital problems in Borneo.

a) Brainstorm the advantages and disadvantages of living in an isolated spot in the tropics.

b) Help students to grasp that all was not well in Millicent's marriage by asking them to speculate why she kept all photographs of her late husband out of sight.

c) This story builds up to a climax when Millicent confesses to murder. Ask students to re-read the story and plot the different steps leading to the climax on a graph.

What do students think of the attitude of the family? Are people today as concerned with what people think as they were in Somerset Maugham's day?

THE YELLOW STREAK

A dramatic story which brings out attitudes towards people of mixed race.

a) This story raises a similar issue to 'The Pool': the problem of mixed marriages and their offspring. Introduce the theme by asking students what the advantages and disadvantages of growing up in a bilingual or bicultural home are today.

b) Izzart's behaviour in this story is governed by the fact that he has a 'yellow streak' or Asian blood. Make sure students understand this and get them to make notes on Izzart's behaviour to Campion, to Willis, when he talks about his school, his mother, and so on.

c) Choose a moral for the story from the following, or invent your own.
   i) Truth will out.
   ii) Only gentlemen behave like gentlemen.
   iii) It is better to accept what you are than to pretend to be what you are not.

## III  The French Riviera Stories
In these stories Somerset Maugham takes a look at the strange collection of characters who inhabit the Riviera playground.

### THE THREE FAT WOMEN OF ANTIBES
A humorous but cruel story about three obsessive dieters and how they give it all up.

a) Introduce the theme with a discussion of people's attitudes to fat people and to thin people, fashions in women's (and men's) figures and so on.

b) Ask students to list the food that they expect the three fat women to be eating. As they read the story, they check if they were right or not.

c) Do diets work? Is it worth dieting? Write a list of 'diet' questions and conduct a class survey.

### THE FACTS OF LIFE
A father gives his son some advice but the son does better by ignoring it. A film of this story (with three others not in this collection) is available commercially on the Rank Video cassette: *Quartet*.

a) Ask students to make notes on the advice a parent might give to a young person leaving home. Role-play the situation in pairs.
b) Ask students to stop reading on p. 210: 'You'll never see that

again.' Will Nicky get his money back or not? Stop again before the last paragraph on p. 213: Is the woman honest or not?

c) Who knows best – parents or children? Was Nicky right to ignore his father's advice or not? Ask students to compare their own experiences.

## GIGOLO AND GIGOLETTE

A story about the depths to which poorer people are pushed to survive in a cruel world.

a) Ask students to describe the most daring stunts they have ever seen on television, at a circus or elsewhere.

b) Stop reading at the bottom of p. 230. Will Syd understand Stella? Will she go on diving or not?

c) What would you do to earn a living if you were desperate?

## THE HAPPY COUPLE

The 'happy couple' have a skeleton in the wardrobe!

a) Brainstorm the ingredients which make a couple 'happy': love, children, money and so on.

b) Stop reading at the bottom of p. 243. Why have the Craigs disappeared? What is their relationship, if any, with Judge Landon?

c) What kind of life do people who escape punishment for crime have? Can they ever forget? Can they be happy?

## THE VOICE OF THE TURTLE

A character sketch of an ageing singer which demonstrates the subjectivity of perception.

a) Brainstorm ideas on how stars behave in private or at home with their families. Are they just like anybody else or are they much more egocentric? Ask students to discuss specific examples that they have read about in the Press (pop stars or Maria Callas – if they have heard of her).

b) Ask students to make two columns in their notebooks. As they read, or after they have finished, they can make notes on Peter Melrose's view of La Falterona and the narrator's view. Is the narrator as biased negatively as Peter Melrose is positively?

c) Write names on the board of a few people who are currently in the news. Divide the class in half. Ask one half to write positive descriptions of them and the other half to write negative descriptions. Exchange papers, read them and discuss the subjectivity of our impressions.

### THE LION'S SKIN

Students may not find the theme of this story, what a 'gentleman' is and how he behaves, particularly relevant to them. They will in any case need to be introduced briefly to the way the class system in England works and the concept of 'gentleman'.

When they have read the story, you can ask them to explain the title of the story by choosing which of the following two proverbs they think Somerset Maugham was probably referring to, giving their reasons:

- A lion's skin is never cheap.
- If the lion's skin cannot, the fox's shall (if force will not solve a problem, cunning will).

### IV  The Spanish Stories

'The Romantic Young Lady', 'The Point of Honour', 'The Mother', 'The Man from Glasgow', 'The Poet', 'The Happy Man' (the last two are treated in more detail in Section I).

Ask students to read these stories as part of a project on what interested, intrigued, fascinated or revolted the narrator, an Englishman, about Spain. Students can work in small groups or pairs on one or two topics. Suggested topics are: men, women, relationships between the sexes, family relationships, behaviour, emotions, the weather, leisure activities, homes, the idea of honour, attitudes to foreigners.

The different contributions could be put together in a classbook and photocopied so that students have their own copy.

A similar project could be carried out on the 'tropical' stories in Section II or on the French Riviera stories in Section III.

### V  Dark Stories

Some of the tropical stories are in a much graver mood than the rest of this collection ('Rain', 'The Pool' and 'Mackintosh'), as is this story set in France.

### THE UNCONQUERED

A grim and moving story set during the German Occupation of France. It is very different in tone from most of the other stories in this collection.

a) Elicit briefly what students know about this period of history. How were Germans perceived by ordinary French people?

b) As they read the story, ask students to keep a record, either in note form or on a graph, of the attitude of Annette's parents to Hans, noticing the change from hostility to friendliness. Stop students reading at the top of p. 307 and ask them whose side they are on. Do they understand the parents' attitude? Do they think Annette is right to remain hostile?

c) Let students read the end of the story. It will probably have considerable impact and further discussion will not be necessary or desirable.

## VI Appearance and Reality

The reference of the title *Appearance and Reality* is to a major work of F. H. Bradley (1846–1924), little known by the general public today. It is a work of the Idealist school, valuing mind over matter.

Analyse and discuss what 'appearance' is and what 'reality' is in this amusing comment on social conventions.

The theme of appearance and reality is omnipresent in this collection of stories. This particular story could be used to introduce an overview session on all the stories. Which are the characters who care for 'reality'? Which are those more interested in 'appearance'?

## VII General activities

### 1 COMPARING

Compare stories for similarities and differences. For example, 'The Fall of Edward Barnard' and 'The Happy Man' (similar themes), the Riviera stories (the kind of people who live there). Students can compare situations, characters, values etc. If you have a mixed ability class, the good readers can read a longer story and the weaker readers a shorter story. They then work together in pairs, to compare the stories.

### 2 MORALITY SCALES

Students are asked to place characters on a morality scale (*see 'The Escape'*). Suggested characters for this activity: Mr Davidson ('Rain'), Hunter Bateman ('The Fall of Edward Barnard'), Captain Forestier ('The Lion's Skin'), Mr Kelada ('Mr Know-All'), Elizabeth Vermont ('The Promise'), Don Pedro ('The Point of Honour'), Ruth and Roger ('The Escape').

## 3  CHARACTERS

a) *Balloon debates*

When the class have read several stories, they choose six to ten characters who they think are most interesting or essential to humanity. They then imagine that all these characters are in a hot-air balloon. The balloon is losing air and two of the characters must give up their place in the balloon so that the rest may survive. In small groups, each student plays the role of one of the characters and pleads his or her case to stay in the balloon. Finally the group votes on who can stay (to avoid deadlock, students are not allowed to vote for themselves). Alternatively, small groups prepare the characters' pleas. Then representatives from each group carry out the balloon debate in front of the whole class. The whole class votes.

b) *The five worst and the five best*

When a number of stories have been read, ask students to choose their five favourite characters and their five worst characters. They compare and justify their choices.

c) *Guess who?*

Ask students to pick out a paragraph describing a character and to memorize the essential details. They then describe the character to a partner. Can he or she identify the character?

d) *A day in the life of . . .*

Write an imaginary day in the life of one of the characters, with some activities that are in character and some which are not. Ask students to spot which are which.

e) *Links*

Students try to link many characters through similarities or differences. Ask a student to describe a character of his or her choice. Then say: 'That makes me think of X because they had a similar problem.' Encourage students to continue the chain of associations of characters until no one can think of any more. For example, the fat women of Antibes might make you think of the fat woman in 'The Luncheon', who in turn might remind you of the selfish nature of La Falterona in 'The Voice of the Turtle'.

f) *Introductions*

Take the first paragraph from several stories. How does Somerset Maugham make us interested in his characters? He often uses the same device for introducing his characters. What is it?

## 4 SUMMARY EXERCISES

Students write their own summaries, or you write an erroneous summary and ask them to spot the mistakes.

## 5 REPORTS

Students can read different stories and report back on them to the whole class. To avoid this being a boring monologue from one student to the teacher, ask them to 'sell' their story to the class, interesting the others and, of course, not giving away any sudden twist at the end of the story. The class gives each student a mark between one and ten, strictly on the criteria: How interesting does that story sound? How much did the speaker make me want to read it?

*Notes prepared by Gillian Porter Ladousse*

# 6   THE RED BADGE OF COURAGE

## *by Stephen Crane*

### *The story*

This is a story of war but not one of glorious actions and heroism. The American Civil War (1861–5) is seen through the eyes of a very young and inexperienced soldier, Henry Fleming (although we do not find out his name until about half-way through the story).

The title means the injury or wound a soldier receives in battle: the loss of blood is a sign of courage. But the courage we see in the story is always doubtful and is treated ironically: the soldiers talk, from the very first page, of 'a brilliant campaign', veterans tell 'tales' of glory. But we see everything as Henry Fleming sees it in simple, realistic detail. This is a psychological vision of the reality of war.

When the battle actually starts, the reality changes completely. Henry's friend Jim dies; Henry already has an injury where another soldier accidentally hit him with the end of his gun. But, psychologically, he cannot face the battle and he runs away and hides in a wood.

At the end of the day he goes back, among the wounded, with his 'red badge of courage' to show, ironically, how brave he was. The next day he is braver in the battle, but feels he is just part of a fighting-machine not a person any more. When his regiment's colours fall he picks them up without thinking and becomes a hero.

Henry Fleming at the beginning was an idealistic young recruit, happy to escape from his studies and march to glory. By the end he has been through all the psychological horrors of war and has no illusions of glory or heroism, just a sense of the tragic waste of it all.

### History

The battle referred to was the Battle of Chancellorsville in Virginia in May 1863. Henry Fleming is on the Northern side, the Union side, against the Confederates, the states which fought to preserve the right to keep slaves.

Stephen Crane had never actually been in battle. His narrative, despite its realism, is intended as a psychological examination of character more than a historic document of American history.

### Level

Although the novel is linguistically quite accessible, it requires a certain psychological maturity in its readers, which might make it most suitable for the sixteen-to-eighteen-year-old age group.

### Point of entry

After this incident, and as he reviewed the battle pictures he had seen, he felt quite competent to return home and make the hearts of the people glow with stories of war. He could see himself in a room of warm tints telling tales to listeners. He could exhibit laurels. They were insignificant; still, in a district where laurels were infrequent, they might shine.

He saw his gaping audience picturing him as the central figure in blazing scenes. And he imagined the consternation and the ejaculations of his mother and the young lady at the seminary as they drank his recitals. Their vague feminine formula for beloved ones doing brave deeds on the battle without risk of life would be destroyed.

This extract (*p. 107, ll. 10–21*) is a good moment to show the difference between the reality of the battle and the way it will be sold: how Henry Fleming himself as the hero of a story of his own telling, and how his listeners want to hear exactly that kind of heroic battle story. This ironic attitude to herosim will be found throughout the novel.

## Presentation and pre-reading stimuli

No actual historical background knowledge of the American Civil War is needed to follow and understand the novel. Indeed it is recommended that any such details be kept until after the reading. Then they can become the subject of a historical research project, once students' interest has been aroused in the tragic and fascinating period. (*See the final section of these notes.*)

The cover illustration gives all the background that is necessary. Where is it set? How can you tell? What war will it be, then? What do students think the title might mean? Note that there is an example of such a 'red badge' on the cover.

## Attitudes and reactions

Attitudes to war will no doubt emerge right from the outset. It is inadvisable to let these develop into panegyrics for pacifism, so use provocative questions like: When can war be justified? What would students fight for? (Don't take 'nothing' for an answer. There usually will be something.) What is bravery, courage? Are the students themselves brave? What would students feel like if they found themselves in a battle, or in any kind of violent situation? Are fear and cowardice natural feelings? Is war a man's business? Would there be no wars if women ruled the world?

Use photographic images of battle (Vietnam, Belsen, Belfast, Beirut, etc.) to elicit opinions on how our impressions and ideas of war are conditioned.

Some or indeed many of these topics should be kept in the forefront of students' minds while they read, and the discussion can continue both during and after the reading of the text.

## Vocabulary and style

Ask students to look out for an ironic tone to the writing from the very beginning: the soldier in the second paragraph who 'developed virtues', for example. The 'trustworthy' nature of his informant, the 'brilliant campaign', and many other touches, insidiously set up expectations in the reader of an attitude to the whole question of soldiering and heroism. They should note the use of similar irony throughout the novel, and some mention of it should be made during almost every lesson. What is its function, in students' opinion? And its effect?

Realistic speech patterns emerge but, in general, should be easy to follow. Vocabulary anticipation on the terminology of uniforms, banners and flags, regiments, weapons and battles will be useful. Much of this will emerge in pre-reading discussion. Students should cope with unknown vocabulary by trying to contextualize it. If a reading diary is kept they should put new vocabulary under such head-ings as: weapons / uniform / army equipment / sounds / sights/ weather / geography / orders / boasting / psychological reactions/ Americanisms or dialect speech/other. In this way, vocabulary can be discussed in class and uncertainties referred to and cleared up quickly.

In the opening pages students will come across several American usages such as the spelling 'rumors' (which in English would be 'rumours'), 'teamster' which means a driver (of a team of horses, originally), 'cracker box' for a biscuit box, 'derned' for damned.

### Reading strategies

There are twenty-four chapters and each of them is very short. The speed of reading will depend on how often the book can be referred to in class. It is recommended that students read three or four chapters a week if possible, and devote at least twenty to thirty minutes of class time a week to discussing the reading and the issues that emerge.

Students should try to sum up each chapter in as few words as possible, indicating the main events of the chapter and the main psychological implications of the chapter. This will allow them to see the plot more clearly and the underlying focus on developing psychological awareness.

### Character psychology

Although the narration is third person and impersonal, there is a gradual closing in on Henry Fleming's own sensations and, indeed, on his identity as a man and as a soldier.

To that extent, this is also a novel of growing up, and students could be invited to make a chart in words under suitable headings of how he grows, moving from 'innocence' through 'growing awareness' to 'experience' and 'self-knowledge', noting also what aspects of his character are tested, and how his own feelings and awareness are tempered, altered and shaped.

A character development graph might be drawn, with the base line indicating the passage of time and actions chapter by chapter, and the upper area charting Henry Fleming's inner development in relation to these outside forces, and the psychological impact of the actions he lives through. Chapter 17, for example, might be one high point of psychological impact, chapters 9 and 19 others.

How does the graph move at the end? Up or down? This might provoke discussion.

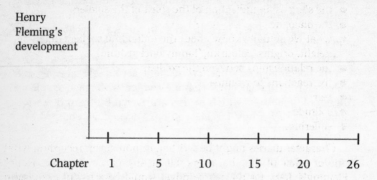

Henry
Fleming's
development

Chapter    1     5    10    15    20    26

### Facts versus feelings

Usually, in making a summary of what has been read, the reader can fix on the facts, the things which actually happen. In this book, feelings and sensations become more significant than the few actual facts narrated. This means that facts can be picked out and recounted, but concentration must be focused on feelings. Use questions like: 'What do you think he feels at this point?', 'What effect does this have on you?', 'What does this description evoke in your own mind?', 'How would you feel in these circumstances?', 'Do you identify with the feelings expressed?', 'How much do you find that this is a realistic description of the scene, or the character's feelings?' etc.

This will shift students' attention from the usual listing of facts and help their involvement with the reading. In order to point out how deliberately vague the author often makes his descriptions, take, for example, chapter 17 (which in any consideration of the novel will be a focal chapter) and have students pick out geographical features and details, or give distances, timings, and so on. These are the kind of details that imply 'realism' but they are very difficult to pin down here. This can open up discussion on what the author actually wants us to see, feel and experience in reading the story. Find out whether students consider this kind of writing more disorienting than documentary description. Why or why not?

### Character

The characters, especially the hero, are given very few identifying traits. Use, for example, chapters 8 and 9 (*pp. 63–72*) to focus on the following ideas:

- the song as an indication of the spirit of the soldiers
- the dialogue
- what we actually know about the individual soldiers (age, height, origins, colouring, family background)
- the relationships between the soldiers
- the reactions to wounds
- fear
- solitude
- suffering.

Character diaries might be written, in note form, recording what one or other of the characters felt at any particular time. Henry Fleming's diary for the whole novel would be a useful exercise in comparing the author's externalized description with his conscious feelings. How much does the reader understand of Henry Fleming's unconscious or subconscious feelings? Is Henry Fleming aware of these feelings himself?

## Documentary

Bring in a newspaper report of a battle or a war from any period (or several different such reports). Then have students prepare a newspaper, radio, or TV report (or all three, done by different groups) of the battles in the novel. Does the reporter have to take a stand on the war or take sides? Is complete objectivity possible? Is it desirable? Why or why not?

## Handling discussion

The issues which come out of this novel are fairly emotive and cannot usually be directly related to students' personal experience. There is, therefore, a strong risk that the discussions become too abstract and theoretical. This can be minimized by keeping close reference to the text or to related materials which the teacher or students introduce. Always bring the discussion back to the text. What is the author's overall intention? What does he want us to feel in this particular scene?, etc. The issue is never as simple as peace versus war.

Contrasts are a feature which will have emerged from the novel (young/old, imagination/reality, innocence/experience, truth at the time/truth after the event, bravery/cowardice etc.). These can be used (and more picked out by students) for before-and-after discussion and evaluation of character development, influence on the reader, reaction and response.

### Research project

If any historical material is available to students in books, encyclopaedias or libraries, this novel is a gift for the preparation of a historical project on the American Civil War. The facts and background are well documented and there are illustrations in many books. In a civil war the phenomenon of brother fighting brother, families divided by the war, and moral standpoints of the individual become very important. *The Red Badge of Courage* is one of many novels about the American Civil War: *Gone with the Wind*, *Uncle Tom's Cabin*, Gore Vidal's *Lincoln* and Walt Whitman's poems in *Leaves of Grass* are all concerned, in various ways, with the war, its causes and its effects.

Have students find out not only the facts but also the feelings and emotions aroused by the Civil War, reactions to it and the artistic representations, including songs and films, it inspired and continues to inspire.

### Final reactions

Oral/written work summing-up: what readers got out of the book, how it reflected or differed from their expectations, how much it is a 'war' story, the 'moral' (if any), whether they would recommend the book to others?

The story 'The Veteran' can be referred to. The hero is called 'the veteran' by others, so the process of myth-making about the events of the war continues. He displays bravery in the traditional sense in this short story. But is it actually foolhardiness? The question must inevitably remain open.

*Notes prepared by John McRae*

## 7  ROBINSON CRUSOE
*by Daniel Defoe*

### Introduction

This book is often considered the first proper novel in English.

Whether or not it is, the story of the solitary man on his desert island has remained one of the most powerful of all myths. The elements of adventure, the fight for survival, the creation of an economic and moral society, and the relationship with Man Friday (one of the first examples of the 'noble savage'), combine to make it a rich and rewarding read, and give endless opportunities for reflection and discussion, which are as relevant today as they were when the book was first published in 1719.

### Fact or fiction?

The narration is in the first person. It is always Robinson Crusoe himself who speaks so the reader is taken right inside the mind and heart of the man. And since the story is based on the well-known true-life story of the Scotsman Alexander Selkirk (1676–1721) who spent five years alone on the uninhabited island of Juan Fernandez – and was still alive when the novel was published – readers are expected to take it as a true story rather than the very clever fiction it actually is.

### The story

The plot is very simple. Crusoe leaves his home in Hull to go to sea and immediately suffers greatly in a storm. This might have been a warning, and should have discouraged him from any further sea adventures. He becomes a trader and his concentration on money (commented on by no less an authority than Karl Marx) will be crucial. By the end of the novel he is a rich man, a typical representative of the new bourgeois culture of the eighteenth century. However, he still has his solo adventure to come. While trading (*pp. 17 ff.*) he is captured and kept prisoner for some two years in what is now Morocco. He eventually manages to escape with a native boy, Xury (an earlier example of the master-slave relationship he will have with Man Friday: although Xury saved Robinson Crusoe's life, he is then sold as a slave for sixty pieces of eight). Crusoe is taken on board a ship heading for 'the Brasils'. Here he makes the business investments which will turn out to provide his future wealth. It is on the voyage back that Crusoe is shipwrecked (*pp. 35–7*) in a very famous scene.

Robinson Crusoe is the only survivor of the shipwreck and he brings ashore (*chapter 4*) goods and utensils – and money (because, as he says, 'upon second thoughts' it might be 'worth saving'). With these he begins to build his life on the island, keeping a count of the days. His ingenuity and spirit are inexhaustible, although he turns to God when he suffers from fever. Otherwise his is the triumph of the individual man over circumstances: he builds a house, grows his food, domesticates animals, makes a boat. In short, he creates a society in miniature for himself alone but clearly on the model of western society. He is 'king' of the island.

When he finds traces of cannibals he becomes very alarmed. The famous vision of 'the print of a man's naked foot on the shore' (*p. 110 and cover illustration*) changes his solitary world and introduces some time later the indigenous native who will save Crusoe's life. Robinson Crusoe calls him Friday, tries to impose his own religion and culture on him, and uses him as a slave: Friday will never be Crusoe's equal. After many adventures – twenty-eight years, two months and nineteen days of them, to be exact (*p. 233*) – Robinson Crusoe is rescued, having quelled a mutiny on board an English ship off his island. He leaves the mutineers to colonize the island and returns to England 'a stranger to all the world'. On the way he discovers that his investments in Brazil have made him a wealthy man and on his return gets married. He goes back to 'my new colony' after his wife's death, and promises further adventures on the now populated and increasingly prosperous island (in the sequel Friday will die) – a far cry from the solitary universe of his stay there when he was king of his own world.

## Level

This can be read from the age of thirteen to fourteen upwards. Younger or newer learners may want to read selected passages rather than the whole novel. The best age level would be sixteen to seventeen.

## Point of entry

It happened one day about noon going towards my boat. I was exceedingly surprised with the print of a man's naked foot on the shore, which was very plain to be seen in the sand. I stood like one thunder-struck, or as if I had seen a ghost; I listened, I looked round me, I could hear nothing, nor see anything; I went up to a rising ground to look farther; I went up the shore and down the shore, but it was all one, I could see no other impression but that one. I went to it again to see if there were any more, and to observe if it might not be my fancy; but there was no room for that, for there was exactly the very print of a foot, toes, heel, and every part of a foot; how it came thither I knew not, nor could in the least imagine. But after innumerable fluttering thoughts, like a man perfectly confused and out of myself, I came home to my fortification, not feeling, as we say, the ground I went on, but terrified to the last degree, looking behind me at every two or three steps, mistaking every bush and tree and fancying every stump at a distance to be a man; nor is it possible to describe how many various shapes affrighted imagination represented things to me in, how many wild ideas were found every moment in my fancy, and what strange unaccountable whimsies came into my thoughts.

The cover can suitably be related to the extract (*p. 110*) as point of entry if students want to sample something of the language, style and tone of the book.

There have been several films of the novel, the most interesting by Luis Buñuel. If any versions are available on video they can be a useful means of comparing Defoe's own style with the externalized presentation of the cinematic version.

### Presentation and pre-reading stimuli

Introduce the story with the name Robinson Crusoe. Have students heard of him? Was he a real person? What do they know about him? Have they heard of Man Friday? What do they know of him? How do they imagine he got his name?

Use the cover illustration to identify the character and situation. Do the students like this image of Robinson Crusoe? How would they prefer to imagine him? Can they suggest the importance of what he has found in the sand?

The theme of a desert island can be presented. Would students enjoy being alone on a desert island? How would they survive? Have them make a list of things they would consider vital for life on the island. Do this under two headings: *Essentials* and *Desirables*. If these lists are done in groups they can then be compared. Usually something terribly important is forgotten!

What would students miss most? And what would they be glad to escape from?

It will be a good idea for students to keep a note of all their answers, suggestions and reactions at this preliminary stage so that they can compare them with what they go on to read, and with their changing reactions and feelings as they read.

### Reading strategies

Because the language is not modern there may be some initial resistance to the style and lexis but do not allow this to impede the reading. (*See the next section for some hints.*)

Reference to reading (while the book is being read) in class time should be chapter by chapter, encouraging the students to read a chapter at a time before it is discussed in class. How much time can be dedicated to this discussion will, of course, depend on the restrictions of the curriculum. Teachers should attempt to make sure that at least twenty minutes a week is devoted to extensive reading otherwise students might lose the rhythm of their reading, or begin to lose track of the story. Encourage, therefore, fairly fast reading, without stopping to check vocabulary except in cases where it is vital for the comprehension of a scene.

### Vocabulary and lexis

Brainstorm vocabulary about ships, storms, a desert island and what would be needed there.

The teacher should pick out a few archaic words or phrases and present them to students in order to familiarize them a little with the style. In the first chapter, for instance, these words could be picked out: nay, befall, chamber, bid (past tense), 'twas, undone.

When students find themselves in difficulty, encourage them to list the unknown words under the headings where they think the word belongs: Archaism (what is the modern equivalent?), Nautical/Technical language (building, agriculture etc.), Other.

In this way vocabulary problems can be aired in class if necessary and discussed in direct relation to the reading.

### Oral summary

To check that chapters have been read, encourage oral summary in class, picking out the details of the story which the students have found most striking so far. Most chapters can be summarized quite effectively in four or five sentences and brevity is to be encouraged.

Discussion can then develop on the features individual students have chosen to focus on. For example, in the opening chapters, one student might give more prominence to the storm and Crusoe's feelings of fear, while another will bring up Crusoe's parents' reactions to his choice of career.

### Discussion points (and summary guidelines)

Possible topics for class discussion or later written work which may emerge include:

- chapter 1  Choosing a career; wanting to leave home; wanting to travel; fear; shipwreck.
- chapter 2  Shame about returning home a failure; uncertainty about the future; his relationship with his captors and with the Moor; is the rescue believable or fantastic?
- chapter 3  Selling Xury – is it a cruel thing to do? or just greedy?; his growing prosperity – why does he speak so much about it?; the shipwreck; how much time has passed already?
- chapter 4  Where did he sleep and why?; his feelings; what he took from the wreck; his attitude to the money; his list of Evil and Good things; his journal.
- chapter 5  How is the narration different?; what he makes and builds; his attitude to God and Heaven; his counting the days.
- chapter 6  His country 'bower'; does he need two places to live? (look at the list of *Essentials*; why do people often want two houses?); 'wants' as opposed to 'needs'; exploring; the kid (a baby goat); his work; the passage of time.
- chapter 7  The boat; the voyage; the parrot – the sound of a voice; his insistence on not being idle – the work ethic.
- chapter 8  The footprint; his apprehensions and defences; the cannibals' feast; his reactions.
- chapter 9  His depression; the cave; the ship; finding more money.
- chapter 10  The canoes; killing the Indian; Friday's first confrontation with the white man; how Crusoe wants to change Friday – starting with how he eats; having to feed two instead of one (a family?); religion.
- chapter 11  The concept of 'nation' – how attached are they to it?; his feelings that he will be rescued; the Spaniard, the old man, and his attitudes to them.
- chapter 12  The subjection of his people – by what right can someone command? ('I was absolute lord and lawgiver'); counting the days.
- chapter 13  His joy at possible rescue; his conditions; the sailors; being 'past the operation of fear' (*p. 212*); treatment of the prisoners.
- chapter 14  The mutineers beg for mercy; the exercise of power/clemency; deliverance, and leaving the island.
- Epilogue  Return, the importance of wealth; the relative unimportance of his marriage; his colonial concerns; the making of a new kind of modern man?; colonial attitudes: the natural superiority of colonizers.

## Handling discussion

Always elicit various points of view. What do students think about the issues rasied? How do the issues in the novel relate to their own lives, experience and concerns? Is Crusoe a psychologically viable character. Do students identify with his feelings and emotions? Where do they no longer share his feelings?

Not necessarily every point listed will provoke discussion, but some wider themes may emerge which can be discussed at various times: the need for a home; the importance of money; the natural environment and being 'close to nature'; is the island a Utopia?; what do students feel about the master/slave relationships with Xury and Friday? And what do they feel about the mutineers who are left to colonize the island?

## Points of view

Since the point of view is always Robinson Crusoe's in the novel, role-play or written work can be done on *different* points of view. Seeing Robinson Crusoe from the point of view, for example, of: Xury; Man Friday; his business partner; Mrs Robinson Crusoe; the Spaniard; the mutineers.

Modern-day attitudes might involve an animal rights activist; an anti-colonialist; a feminist.

## Desert islands then and now

Class debates or written work can be organized, arguing for or against the following:

- Robinson Crusoe was right to treat Friday as he did. It was his duty to civilize him.
- Robinson Crusoe was a nasty bourgeois capitalist.
- Robinson Crusoe shows the worst side of colonial imperialism.
- The story is more truth than fiction.
- Nowadays it is always 'Girl Friday' (to mean a secretary, or a manager's personal assistant) rather than 'Man Friday'. Is this indicative of men's attitudes to women?
- The island was a kind of paradise.
- Today desert islands are only exploited for business and tourism.
- Robinson Crusoe is every one of us.
- If Crusoe had been a woman she would have managed better.
- Truth and fiction in the 'myth' of Robinson Crusoe.

*Desert Island Discs*
Like the BBC radio programme, what eight pieces of music and what three books or videos would you take with you to your desert island?

*Geography*
Find in an atlas all the places mentioned and draw a map of Robinson Crusoe's various voyages. Where is his island?

Make a map of his island, incorporating all the geographical features one by one as they appear in the story.

*Notes prepared by John McRae*

# 8   DRACULA

## *by Bram Stoker*

### *The story*

The story of Count Dracula is based on old legends of Transylvania (present-day Romania). The tall thin Count, with his sharp nose, pointed ears and animal-like teeth, lives by sucking the blood of humans. He is the original vampire! He sleeps by day in boxes like coffins filled with earth and by night he goes in search of his victims who remain Un-Dead until a stake is driven through their hearts.

We read about Count Dracula in the diaries, letters and journals of the people he encounters and torments. So the point of view changes frequently and the style is immediate and very personal. Dracula is always presented as a figure of mystery and horror and there is no attempt to see his point of view or to present him with sympathy.

Jonathan Harker travels to Castle Dracula, and there begins his horrific experiences, culminating in the discovery in a ruined chapel of the Un-Dead Count lying in an earth-filled box, having gorged himself with blood. The action then moves to England – Count Dracula buys an estate in Essex – and Dracula arrives in the shape of a wolf, having vampirized the entire crew of the ship he was travelling on. Almost immediately, Jonathan's fiancée Mina and her friend Lucy are at risk. Despite many blood transfusions and Professor Van Helsing's occult intervention, Lucy becomes Dracula's victim.

Dracula's boxes filled with earth must be neutralized, using religious means. But Dracula, after trying hard to suck Mina's blood,

137

escapes back to Transylvania in the last of the fifty boxes he brought with him. There is an exciting chase and Dracula is finally beheaded, a stake driven through his heart and his body turns to dust.

## Level
Style and content both suggest that students should have a certain level of maturity for reading *Dracula*. Sixteen to seventeen year olds and older students will probably be able to get most out of it.

## Style
The diary form means that the text can be read easily and quickly in fairly short sections. The late Victorian period (the novel was first published in 1897) is brought to life in train journeys across Europe, in the evocation of the mysterious Transylvania contrasting with the peace and normality of the English countryside, in the roles the men and women play (the men are defenders, the women victims, for the most part), and in what have become stereotypes: the slightly mad Professor, the vapid heroine, the virginal victim, the agonizingly normal hero, and so on.

How much these are stereotypes, and how convincing students find them, can be gone into during and after the reading.

## Point of entry

'We are in Transylvania; and Transylvania is not England. Our ways are not your ways, and there shall be to you many strange things. Nay, from what you have told me of your experiences already, you know something of what strange things here may be.'

As the door began to open, the howling of the wolves without grew louder and angrier; their red jaws, with champing teeth, and their blunt-clawed feet as they leaped, came in through the opening door. I knew that to struggle at the moment against the Count was useless. With such allies as these at his command, I could do nothing. But still the door continued slowly to open, and only the Count's body stood in the gap. Suddenly it struck me that this might be the moment and the means of my doom; I was to be given to the wolves, and at my own instigation. There was a diabolical wickedness in the idea great enough for the Count, and as a last chance I cried out:–

These two passages might be used to give readers something of the flavour of this book. The first (*p 32, ll. 14–18*) underlines the whole mysterious and different nature of Transylvania. The second (*p. 65, ll. 19–30*) gives a classic moment of creaking doors, howling wolves and impending doom. (But since it is all narrated in the first person perhaps there is the reassurance that everything will work out all right in the end.)

## Presentation and pre-reading stimuli

Start from the name. What do students know of *Dracula*? Have they seen the film or even *The Rocky Horror Show*? What about vampires? Do they really exist? Where do students get any knowledge they have of these things: movies, cartoons, TV, videos?

Use the cover illustration to put into words the description of the figure of Dracula, finding adjectives to describe his smile, his skin colour, his hair, his cloak, etc.; and to discuss how apposite this image is and how it has been represented visually in movies etc.

Stress this is the original story of Dracula and elicit what students think it will be about and what 'horrors' it will involve.

## Vocabulary

It will be necessary to have a preliminary session on the vocabulary of horror. Bring out all the possible adjectives to do with fear, horror, anxiety, terror, etc. And also the nouns and verbs associated with blood-sucking, biting, preying, coffins, religious ceremonies, crosses, crypts and chapels. Bring out the importance of the connotations of these words, which will almost always be negative in this novel. Religious words especially, which would normally have fairly positive connotations, are here shaded negatively. Corruption is another semantic area to be explored. Students should build up a reading diary where they can write in unknown words, putting them under headings where they think they belong: death /-corruption / vampires / terror / science / travel/ property / religion / superstition / other.

## Genre

The horror story as a genre can be examined either using this single example, or widening the scope to include, for example, Robert Louis Stevenson's *Doctor Jekyll and Mr Hyde*, Edgar Allan Poe's *Tales of Mystery and Imagination* and Mary Shelley's *Frankenstein*. Discussion might focus on the following topic areas: why do people like horror stories?; what is actually frightening, if anything?; is there any psychological truth in the characters and their preoccupation?; are modern equivalents (Stephen King, James Her-

bert, and movies of their work) more or less effective than the
'traditional' stories?; why do some people want to laugh at the
whole thing?

## *Group reading*

If the length of the book is a problem, either in terms of reading
time, or of student motivation, divide the class into three (or four)
groups, who will read separate sections and report back on them.
Suggested sections: chapters 1–4, 5–9, 10–13, 14–18, 19–22,
23–7 (three groups, two sections each).

Students in each group must make clear notes on their chapters
which give the other groups a clear idea of: who is narrating;
which characters are involved; where they are; what they are
doing, seeing and thinking; the most significant horror scenes;
what they think will happen next.

If students are encouraged to visualize each scene cinematically,
role-play or acting out of some scenes can be built in as part of the
reporting-back procedure. Students must be told to skim fairly
quickly through the chapters they are not actually concentrating
on, and to make notes from their colleagues' reports on these
scenes, interrupting and asking questions during the reporting-
back lessons.

Cinematic techniques can include: close-ups (usually of Dracula
and his victims); long-shots (to show landscapes, or to create an
atmosphere of mystery in the corridors and depths of the castle);
special effects (bite marks, scientific/religious experiments, coffins,
stake through the heart, etc.), dialogue (which can be modernized,
abbreviated, invented, according to the group's interpretation and
requirements). It will always be important to stick fairly close to a
basic summary of the action of the chapters being examined: it
would be too easy to fly off into exaggerated realms of fantasy.
This can be done, if the mood of the class is right, only after the
complete reading of the text, when there is a clear, objective view
of the plot and structure of the whole novel, rather than
enthusiasm for some single scenes or special effects.

After the complete reading, a cinema version can be structured.
Which scenes would be left out and why? How much dialogue
would there be? How many special effects? Would students want
to take any moral attitudes or draw any moral conclusions in
the movie?

## *Characters*

There is plenty of scope for character study in this novel. Students can make up a 'personality dossier' of single characters: the Count, Jonathan Harker, Lucy, Mina, Professor Van Helsing, and several of the more minor characters.

One game is to find a suitable adjective for each character: 'staid' for Harker, 'dangerous' for Dracula, for example, and during the reading build up the number and range of adjectives used. Try for up to six different adjectives for each character.

The personality of the character built up in this way should cover headings like: age and social status; profession; relationships; strengths and weaknesses of character; changes the character undergoes during the story; final destiny (predictions and result). Which actor or actress would students chose to play the character in a present-day movie?

### What if?

A game to exercise students' imagination, with some grammar work thrown in.

- What if Jonathan hadn't gone to Transylvania?
- What if Count Dracula hadn't wanted to buy property in England?
- What if Van Helsing had been *more* successful?
- What if Van Helsing had been *less* successful?
- What if Lucy had lived?
- What if Dracula had got Mina?
- What if none of the fifty boxes had been left?, and so on.

### True or false?

This is useful for checking details in the reading, during class or group reporting-back sessions. It can be expanded also to cover aspects of interpretation. Students can go on to invent their own questions along these lines:

- Dracula's victims are always women.
- Jonathan Harker is more fascinated than frightened by Dracula.
- Most of the characters don't care about death.
- Van Helsing is not very intelligent.
- The Un-Dead are still walking the earth.
- Dracula was not the 'great dog' on the ship.
- Dracula really existed.
- Lucy is perfectly healthy.
- Transylvania is a real place.

- A vampire can be killed by stabbing it with a knife.
- Lucy is buried beside her mother, and so on.

### Geography
Use of a map of Europe to trace the characters' travels across Europe, to England by ship, within England, and back to Transylvania. This map can be consulted at all times, and a geographical log of the characters' movements kept throughout the reading. Plans of the castle and of various other localities can be drawn up also. These will be especially useful if there is to be a cinematic or video version, or if scenes are to be role-played after the reading.

### The Dracula home-made video
This can be done with video equipment or just acted out as if a video were being made. Divide the class into groups of eight to ten students. It is important that each member of each group has a clear role to play. Roles: director, cameraman, Dracula, Harker, Van Helsing, the ship's crew, Lucy, Mina, Quincey Morris, (other friends in England), Dr Seward.

Each group should decide on a maximum of four or five scenes to act out (scenes can overlap between different groups), make a written summary of the events to give a plot line, then prepare a shooting script (with a description of the visual aspects, the characters' movements, the camera movements and, last but not least, some dialogue). Make-up and props are left to the teacher's and the class's discretion and inventiveness. If possible, some rehearsal should be done in students' own time to avoid too much upheaval in class.

The video can be done extremely quickly in one lesson of class time or fleshed out into a full-scale drama project. Be careful that it doesn't turn into a re-run of *The Rocky Horror Show*.

*Notes prepared by John McRae*

## 9   THE ADVENTURES OF TOM SAWYER

*by Mark Twain*

### The story
The tale of Tom Sawyer and his friends is set in St Petersburg, Missouri, on the river Mississippi, in about the middle of the last century. Tom has a series of adventures, usually hilarious, as when

he gives the cat medicine (*pp. 85–6*). But many other things happen too: Tom and his friend Huckleberry Finn witness the murder of the town's doctor by Injun Joe. After the murder a drunk man is accused because Injun Joe put the weapon, a knife, in his hands.

Tom and Huck run away to an island on the river after Becky, Tom's girlfriend, treats him coldly. Everyone thinks that they are dead. When they come back, they find their funeral in progress!

Then Tom saves Muff Jones, the drunk man, with his revelation of the truth. The Indian escapes but is found when Tom and Becky get lost. What will Injun Joe do to his enemy, Tom? What will happen to the Indian's buried treasure? And will Huck Finn ever wash and become a normal civilized person?

Funny and exciting, thrilling and involving, this is the classic American childhood story, full of character and incident, creating an unforgettable world, and leading on to the story of *Huckleberry Finn*.

## Narration

The story is narrated in the third person, but right from the first chapter it is clear that the narrator's sympathies, and therefore the reader's sympathies too, are intended to lie with Tom. So characters like Tom's aunt, the unnamed 'she' (*p. 7*) revealed as Aunt Polly on the next page, are in a sense seen through Tom's eyes as people to be played tricks on, as the opposition. They are grown-ups and a great part of a successful reading of this book will depend on seeing the adult/boy conflict as the pretext for much of Tom's behaviour.

A good example, right at the beginning of the book, is the 'look behind you' trick Tom plays on his Aunt Polly (*p. 8*). Of course there is no malice involved, as can be seen from her line, 'Can't I ever learn anything', and her laughter at being taken in. Laughter is largely what the book is about, and when it touches on serious themes (murder, slavery, Tom's death), the reader is always reassured that nothing bad will actually happen.

This is Twain's re-creation of the free spirit of childhood: more than a narratorial point of view, it involves the reader in a kind of conspiracy with Tom, in which we know that everything will turn out all right, despite the machinations of aunts, murderers and others who would destroy the innocent mischievousness of Tom Sawyer.

## Level

There is a fair amount of colloquial and dialect speech used, so although the ideal reading age might be thirteen to fourteen years old, students would be more comfortable with the story at the ages of fifteen to sixteen.

If the students are mainly girls, the book might not go down as well as it would with a class of boys or a mixed group.

## Point of entry

Tom felt that it was time to wake up; this sort of life might be romantic enough in his blighted condition, but it was getting to have too little sentiment and too much distracting variety about it. So he thought over various plans for relief, and finally hit upon that of professing to be fond of Pain-killer. He asked for it so often that he became a nuisance, and his aunt ended by telling him to help himself and quit bothering her. If it had been Sid she would have had no misgivings to alloy her delight; but since it was Tom she watched the bottle clandestinely. She found that the medicine did really diminish, but it did not occur to her that the boy was mending the health of a crack in the sitting-room floor with it.

One day Tom was in the act of dosing the crack when his aunt's yellow cat came along, purring, eyeing the tea-spoon avariciously, and begging for a taste. Tom said:

'Don't ask for it unless you want it, Peter.'

But Peter signified that he did want it.

'You better make sure.'

Peter was sure.

'Now you've asked for it, and I'll give it to you, because there ain't anything mean about *me*; but if you find you don't like it you mustn't blame anybody but your own self.'

Peter was agreeable, so Tom pried his mouth open and poured down the Pain-killer. Peter sprang a couple of yards into the air, and then delivered a war-whoop and set off round and round the room, banging against furniture, upsetting flower-pots, and making general havoc. Next he rose on his hind feet and pranced around, in a frenzy of enjoyment, with this head over his shoulder and his voice proclaiming his unappeasable happiness. Then he went tearing around the house again, spreading chaos and destruction in his path. Aunt Polly entered in time to see him throw a few double summersets, deliver a final mighty hurrah, and sail through the open window, carrying the rest of the flower-pots with him. The old lady stood petrified with astonishment, peering over her glasses; Tom lay on the floor, expiring with laughter.

'Tom, what on earth ails that cat?'
'*I* don't know, Aunt,' gasped the boy.

One of the most comic moments might be used to introduce readers to the novel: the dosing of Peter the cat with the Pain-killer (*pp. 85–6*). The actual effects are described on p. 86 in the first long paragraph, but the complete episode could be read from p. 85, l. 16 until Tom's innocent '*I* don't know, Aunt' on p. 86.

Tom's false innocence, his relationship with his Aunt and the basically harmless sense of fun in the passage should all be attractive to readers. And the cat's antics would make even a cat laugh.

## Presentation and pre-reading stimuli

Use the cover to find out what kind of person the illustration shows. Would students like him and get on with him? What kind of adventures do they think the book will recount? Where do students think the story will be set? Why? Is the kind of boat shown familiar?

In order to get the flavour of the book and to be able to handle some of the vocabulary and dialect questions immediately, some teachers might like to begin by reading in class (or for the students to read at home, but to go through in class afterwards) the famous whitewashing episode from 'Tom appeared . . .' (*p. 15, l. 6*) to 'bankrupted every boy in the village' (*p. 19 eighth last line*). (*See the next section.*) What do students expect the verb 'to whitewash' will mean literally?

Many of the tricks can be used for prediction along these lines: Tom wants to get out of whitewashing the fence. How do you think he will do it? Later this can cover the more serious questions such as 'How do you think Tom and Huck will manage to see justice is done after the murder?'

## Dialect and dialogue

Twain uses Tom's language, his thoughts and attitudes, expressed in his own words, so, inevitably, the reader entering into Tom's world will be involved in 'learning' his language. Let us take the whitewashing episode, mentioned above, as the key to these questions of dialogue and dialect. First of all, there are American usages, such as 'side-walk' (pavement) and unusual words such as 'mulatto' (a person of mixed race). Point these out and give students the task of noting down in a reading diary any vocabulary that is more commonly found in American rather than British English.

A second vocabulary section in the students' reading diary might be 'spoken' as opposed to 'written' language. Examples could include 'gals' (girls) and 'gimme' (give me) (*p. 15*).

Perhaps what is most likely to cause problems is a mixture of these elements, that is, spoken American. And here we have to distinguish between Tom's language and, for example, the words spoken by the negro slave, Jim, as in the second last paragraph on p. 15. In order to accustom students to these varied speech renditions a *transcription* exercise can be helpful: writing the dialogue in more normal English forms. Jim's first paragraph might come out something like this:

*'I can't, Master Tom. Old Mrs (my old mistress) told me I have got to go and get this water and I have not to stop and play (around) with anybody. She said she expected Master Tom was going to ask me to whitewash, and she told me to go along and attend to my own business – she allowed (said) that she would attend to the white-washing.'*

This paragraph contains the vast majority of speech problems that students will come across during their reading. Have them point out where they find: extra, omitted or wrongly placed pronouns; wrong tenses; words which *sound* almost correct, but which are written strangely ('Mas'r' and 'tole', for example); consonantal confusion ('d' for 'th' is the most common); words which look completely new but actually represent quite familiar concepts ('gwyne' for 'going to', 'spec' for '(I) expect', and 'ax' for 'ask' recur frequently).

This kind of familiarization exercise should be treated as an enjoyable one. Relate it to songs that students might have heard and to usages they have found in pop lyrics, as well as to dialect forms in their own language. Stress the universality of the phenomenon and, therefore, the inventiveness of Twain in his rendering of a range of speech patterns.

Thus, when Ben Rogers hoves into view in his role as a Mississippi steamboat, his conversation can be similarly tackled and will be found to be rather easier to handle: 'stabboard' and 'labboard' are starboard and its opposite, larboard (or port), indicating the sides of the boat Ben is announcing himself to be (have students say what other words are probably just Ben's idea of nautical terminology – 'gauge-cocks', for example); 'up a stump' is an idiomatic expression meaning, more or less, in a difficult position, Tom's 'warn't' is his usual form for wasn't, 'you'd druther' is

146

you would rather, and, of course, 'ain't' is isn't. Don't take up too much time on this as the trick and Tom's calculated victory are to be enjoyed rather than battled through. Students should find this careful clarification motivating in terms of their being able to enjoy the story.

## Summary

After reading about the trick, ask students for a very brief summary of how Tom achieved his aim. This can be oral or written, although it is advisable to begin with an oral summary in class. A one-sentence summary, without names and details, is a useful technique to develop. For example, in just a few words: 'He managed to convince the others that whitewashing the fence was exactly what they really wanted to do'. This kind of very short summary can go into students' readers diaries to remind them of various scenes and also to show how simply they can render quite a complex scene. More detailed summaries can be built up by going round the class, inviting each student to contribute one salient fact, item or detail in going over the chapter or scene they have read. But it is counter-productive to try to get every detail in! It is always better to put a length limit on any summary.

## Vocabulary and register

In the whitewashing scene some of Twain's register variations and their effects can be brought out. Take, for example, the sentence (*p. 15, ll. 10–11*): 'It seemed to him that life was hollow, and existence but a burden.' This is a good example of the gentle irony and exaggerated seriousness that Twain employs to underline Tom's state of mind. The style and register become a little more elevated ('but a burden') and literary, and the contrast between Tom's simpler expression and this narratorial aside underline the comic intent of the scene.

Students will easily find more exaggerations: 'a deep melancholy' and 'the far-reaching continent of unwhitewashed fence' might be pointed out. Once this concept has been introduced, students should be on the lookout for it throughout the novel. 'Tom girded up his loins' (*p. 26*), for instance, uses a biblical phrase, meaning 'he prepared himself'. The contrast between the biblical register and the task he prepares himself for allows a moment of comic insight. Particularly striking, pleasing or humorous examples of this can be noted in the students' reading diaries.

Unusual vocabulary can be handled in many different ways. In chapter 2 words like 'playthings' are likely to be unfamiliar, but should not present difficulties, while 'skylarking' should be related precisely to Jim's 'foolin' 'roun'. Encourage students to read on without worrying too much about unknown words. Where they do look up words in their dictionaries, these should be noted in their reading diaries.

For the actual whitewashing, preliminary brainstorming on the lines of: 'What would you need to whitewash a large fence' should elicit such items as brush, pail and so on. This can also be done after a first rapid reading of the opening paragraph, asking students to pick out words which must be concerned with the painting of the fence.

### Tom's tricks

Encourage students, as they read, to make a list of Tom's tricks played on other people, right from the very first page. In this way some of the major elements of the story, such as the return of the boys during the funeral service (*chapter 18, pp. 116–19*), might come to be evaluated as *unintentional* tricks, while the whitewashing is a deliberate one.

Students should also list events under headings of 'Tom in control' and 'Tom not in control'. An example of the latter might be in chapter 10, and the letter Tom and Huck write (*p. 74*) as they try to get things back under their control.

Practical joking might be a good subject for role-play and discussion. What practical jokes have students played or heard of? These can be acted out, as long as chaos does not result!

### Discussion

Tom Sawyer does not offer the range of discussion topics that its sequel, *Huckleberry Finn*, gives. But, in passing, it does raise a number of issues which could develop into class discussion. For example: the acceptance of the roles of coloured people as slaves; the limits of the authority of parents (or guardians, as here); what would you do if you saw a murder? If the class is not used to open discussion, the subjects can be prepared beforehand. Three or four students should be ready with a few sentences outlining their views, and the others encouraged to challenge, contradict, agree. They should contribute their own opinions on and reactions to the subject *and* to what others have said about it.

As the class becomes more used to this kind of discussion, other fields can be opened up (the place of the church in this society; how bad was Injun Joe?; what Tom and Huck should have done at the time of the murder, etc.) and if students go on to *Huckleberry Finn* a whole series of concerns can be brought into the discussion.

### What if?
An exercise in imagination, with some grammar practice too.

- What if Muff Jones had not been there just after the murder?
- What if Injun Joe had killed Tom and Huck?
- What if the cat had enjoyed the medicine?
- What if Becky had wanted to go with Tom?
- What if they had not come back during the funeral service?
- What if Aunt Polly had been very severe?
- What if Tom and Becky had not got lost?
- What if they had not turned up again?
- What if Injun Joe had not died?, and so on.

### Boys will be boys
Young female readers do not usually take to Tom and Huck. This reaction could be used to bring out differences in attitudes and behaviour for discussion or written work, but, preferably, not for heated argument! For example, girls would not try to play all these tricks on other girls; there is more solidarity than competition between girls; girls would not carry around a dead cat, like Huck, or give a cat medicine, like Tom; boys tend to be dirtier; girls would give more consideration to what other people thought, and to how people would worry about them.

If the class divides into factions, the male contingent might like to reply with suggestions like: boys are much more independent and adventurous; boys have more imagination; it was Becky who turned out to be weaker when they got lost; girls are soppy and squeamish.

Of course, the class might react more polemically: are the roles of boys and girls described in the novel outdated? Is Twain affirming a concept of male supremacy? Is he sexist? Is he racist? Are Tom and Huck racist? Is the village integrated, bigoted or too idealized?

Is this just a boys' story in the way *Anne of Green Gables* is a girls' story? Do these distinctions carry over into adult writing (Westerns and spy stories against romances and historical novels)?

Have the girls in the class present Becky's point of view with regard to Tom at some of their key moments together. For example, when she has 'stopped coming to school' (p. 83) and being lost (pp. 192–8). Others can collaborate on the reasons behind their 'wanting to come' and Tom's 'independence' from Becky (pp. 124–5). Do they ever see Tom as 'a glittering hero' (p. 151)?

## *True or false?*

This is a good way of checking that students have read and understood the text. It can be used round the class, each student suggesting a fact, which the others have to decide is true or false. Frequently facts will have to be checked against the text. For example:

- Holler Nuff is one of Tom's friends. (It actually is a phrase meaning 'shout "enough" ' for example, 'I give in' in a fight.)
- Ben Rogers whitewashed most of the fence.
- Muff Rogers witnessed the murder.
- Tom and Huck are cousins.
- Becky Thatcher's brother is called Jeff.
- Aunt Polly is religious.
- Becky's father is a lawyer.
- Aunt Polly does not always forgive Tom.
- The schoolmaster punishes his pupils very cruelly.
- The treasure originally belonged to Murrel's gang.
- Injun Joe tries to kill the Widow Douglas.
- Tom got lost with Becky deliberately.
- McDougal's cave was known as a dangerous place.

## *Special effects*

Added to Twain's playing with register is his use of special graphological effects. The letter (*p. 74*) is one of the best-known. It could be used before students read the chapter with questions like: 'What do you think they are to keep quiet about? Who wrote the letter? What spelling or grammar mistakes are there in it? Why do you think it is written like this in the text?

Other graphological effects are on p. 38: Why are the two lines printed like this? What is the effect *before* you read what is happening, and *after* you know what is happening?; p. 36: Why are the words 'David and Goliath' in capital letters?; p. 51: Why is the third line in capital letters? And why are '*the only vacant place*' and '*girls*' in italics at l. 1 and l. 16?; on pp. 139–40 why are the two stanzas of the poem presented as they are? Is it a good poem? How can you tell? Why are the words 'interesting' and 'poem' in inverted commas in the lines immediately preceding the poem? Are the reasons the same for 'A Vision' being set in smaller letters on p. 140?; on p. 166 why are there 'stage directions' in square brackets (ll. 5–8)?

### Humour and adventure

There are heroes of adventure, like Robin Hood (*p. 160*) and Guy of Guisborne (*p. 64*), mentioned in the story. Have students find out about them from encyclopaedias if these names are unfamiliar. Why do students think they are mentioned? What do such names mean to Tom and Huck? Do they see themselves as heroes?

Do Tom and Huck have a sense of humour? Do students find their adventures funny in themselves? If not, what makes the book funny?

### Conclusions

After reading the whole book, have students discuss, then perhaps write out, their reactions to the story. Was it enjoyable/difficult, exciting/silly, old-fashioned/true-to-life? Encourage them to refer to the text in all their statements.

Would they recommend the book to others? Why or why not? Would they like to go on to the sequel *Huckleberry Finn*?

*Notes prepared by John McRae*

## 10   THE ADVENTURES OF HUCKLEBERRY FINN

### *by Mark Twain*

### The story

This book continues the story of *Tom Sawyer*, with some of the same characters, but it soon becomes a different kind of 'adventure'. It is narrated in the first person by Huckleberry Finn himself, who is now fourteen years old. The narration reflects his ungrammatical speech patterns, his attitudes – both wise and innocent – and the concerns of his time: slavery and life on the frontier of expanding mid-century America.

Huck runs away to escape from his father, who only wants his treasure. With Jim, the negro slave, Huck begins to sail down river (Jim has been accused of murdering Huck, so they can't go back home). After an accident, they are separated and end up first with feuding slave families and then with two crooks, the 'King' and the 'Duke'. These two swindlers sell Jim as a slave. Huck determines to rescue Jim and his old friend Tom Sawyer turns up. Here some fun ensues and then the 'King' and the 'Duke' are punished. Jim has been freed by his old owner, Miss Watson, on her death. Tom could have told Huck earlier, but, mischievously, he wanted the 'adventure'. This shows the rather cruel side to Tom's character.

Tom's and Huck's worlds don't really coincide but their worlds, and Jim's, are indicative of the tensions between 'civilized' America, new frontier America and the world of black people, then still called 'niggers'.

The story turns out to be a moral tale of using people, of respecting the rights of others, and a celebration (with many ambiguities) of the nature of freedom.

## Level

This book should really be read after *Tom Sawyer*. It is rather more difficult, in terms of style, language and content, and so it is recommended for the final years and for students whose language level is good.

## Language, style and narration

The author's 'Notice' (*p. 5*), although comic in tone is worth more than a glance. Twain tries to disclaim the traditional elements of the novel, notably the plot, to make the reader feel that the narrative is really Huck's. This is not unlike the kind of disclaimer Daniel Defoe gives in *Robinson Crusoe* and in other novels too, pretending his fiction is real and the narration a true story.

Realism is very much part of Twain's aim in this novel and, as a consequence, the comic aspects of the tale are much less evident than they are in *Tom Sawyer*, where there are many comic set-pieces. None the less there are several comic scenes and the overall tone, though touching on potentially tragic questions, remains comic to the end. Twain does not want to upset the status quo of the America he describes; but he does present it with its many faults. Chapter 22, when Colonel Sherburn subdues the lynch mob, perhaps shows best Twain's *un*comic vision, his fairly pessimistic outlook on humanity – a vision which can be seen to contain a degree of cynicism.

The 'Explanatory' note (*p. 6*) shows some of his seriousness of intent with regard to language and dialect. For in the eight years or so since the completion of *Tom Sawyer* in 1876 (*Huckleberry Finn* was first published in Britain in 1884, in America in 1885), Twain had been deeply involved in noting down and transcribing various mid-American dialects. This is, indeed, one of the features for which he became most famous: he was among the first writers to document the development of the American language.

Twain also goes further with narrative techniques in this novel than he had gone before. It is narrated by Huck in his own idiolect, or personal language, and, in technical terms, his narration anticipates what was to become known as the 'stream of consciousness', a few years after this novel was published. Obviously each teacher will decide how much stress is to be laid on this kind of technical feature. It can be kept as simple as 'Huck's narration flows just like the Mississippi which flows constantly through the novel' or it can be examined stylistically in relation to other similar narrations.


### Point of entry

Two or three days and nights went by; I reckon I might say they swum by, they slid along so quiet and smooth and lovely. Here is the way we put in the time. It was a monstrous big river down there – sometimes a mile and a half wide; we run nights, and laid up and hid day-times; soon as night was most gone, we stopped navigating and tied up – nearly always in the dead water under a tow-head; and then cut young cotton-woods and willows and hid the raft with them. Then we set out the lines. Next we slid into the river and had a swim, so as to freshen up and cool off; then we set down on the sandy bottom where the water was about knee-deep, and watched the daylight come. Not a sound anywheres – perfectly still – just like the whole world was asleep, only sometimes the bullfrogs a-clattering, maybe. The first thing to see, looking away over the water, was a kind of dull line – that was the woods on t'other side – you couldn't make nothing else out; then a pale place in the sky; then more paleness, spreading around; then the river softened up, away off, and warn't black any more, but grey; you could see little dark spots drifting along, ever so far away – trading-scows, and such things; and long black streaks – rafts; sometimes you could hear a sweep screaking; or jumbled-up voices, it was so still, and sounds come so far; and by-and-by you could see a streak on the water which you know by the look of the streak that there's a snag there in a swift current which breaks on it and makes that streak look that way; and you see the mist curl up off of the water, and the east reddens up, and the river, and you make out a log cabin in the edge of the woods, away on the bank on t'other side of the river, being a wood-yard, likely, and piled by them cheats so you can throw a dog through it anywheres; then the nice breeze springs up, and comes fanning you from over there, so cool and fresh, and sweet to smell, on account of the woods and the flowers; but sometimes not that way, because they've left dead fish laying around, gars, and such, and they do get pretty rank; and next you've got the full day, and everything smiling in the sun, and the song-birds just going it!

'Why,' says he, 'a magician could call up a lot of genies, and they would hash you up like nothing before you could say Jack Robinson. They are as tall as a tree and as big around as a church.'

'Well,' I says, 's'pose we got some genies to help *us* – can't we lick the other crowd then?'

'How you going to get them?'

'I don't know. How do *they* get them?'

'Why, they rub an old tin lamp or an iron ring, and then the genies come tearing in, with the thunder and lightning a-ripping around and the smoke a-rolling, and everything they're told to do they up and do it. They don't think nothing of pulling a shot-tower up by the roots, and belting a Sunday-school superintendent over the head with it – or any other man.'

'Who makes them tear around so?'

'Why, whoever rubs the lamp or the ring. They belong to whoever rubs the lamp or the ring, and they've got to do whatever he says. If he tells them to build a palace forty miles long, out of di'monds, and fill it full of chewing-gum, or whatever you want, and fetch an emperor's daughter from China for you to marry, they've got to do it – and they've got to do it before sun-up next morning too. And more – they've got to waltz that palace around over the country wherever you want it, you understand.'

'Well,' says I, 'I think they are a pack of flatheads for not keeping the palace themselves 'stead of fooling them away like that. And what's more – if I was one of them I would see a man in Jericho before I would drop my business and come to him for the rubbing of an old tin lamp.'

'How you talk, Huck Finn. Why, you'd *have* to come when he rubbed it, whether you wanted to or not.'

'What, and I as high as a tree and as big as a church? All right, then: I *would* come; but I lay I'd make that man climb the highest tree there was in the country.'

'Shucks, it ain't no use to talk to you, Huck Finn. You don't seem to know anything, somehow – perfect sap-head.'

I thought all this over for two or three days, and then I reckoned I would see if there was anything in it. I got an old tin lamp and an iron ring and went out in the woods and rubbed and rubbed till I sweat like an Injun, calculating to build a palace and sell it; but it warn't no use, none of the genies come. So then I judged that all that stuff was only just one of Tom Sawyer's lies. I reckoned he believed in the A-rabs and the elephants, but as for me I think different. It had all the marks of a Sunday-school.

The real point of entry to this book is *Tom Sawyer*. But a scene which might be used is the opening of chapter 19 (*pp. 118–19*), a long paragraph which gives the idea of the river, the hiding, the calm of the runaways and a clear idea of Huck's language and attitudes.

Tom Sawyer's 'lies' (*pp. 22–3*), with the story of the genie's lamp, might be a useful link with the previous novel for those who want to remind themselves of the atmosphere of that book.

### Presentation and pre-reading stimuli

Reading *Huckleberry Finn* will be a more serious undertaking than reading *Tom Sawyer*. This in no way means that the reading should be onerous. If students enjoyed *Tom Sawyer* this novel should be introduced as a deeper, richer and more rewarding exploration of not dissimilar fictional territory.

Presentation should begin with the students' recall of *Tom Sawyer*. What characters, places and events do they remember? Find out what they enjoyed most about that story. The first page of *Huckleberry Finn* takes up the very end of the earlier novel: the treasure, the widow, and how the money was used (*see chapter 36*), so that the direct connection is made.

What do students expect to be different and what the same in this novel? Anticipate that Huck is the narrator. How do they see him in relation to Tom? Older? wiser? More adventurous? Does the cover reflect their ideas of Huck? If not, what should he be like?

Some teachers might like to face up to the novel's problem areas before the reading gets under way. The word 'niggers' can be a useful starting-point. It is first used in relation to Jim, who will be one of the most important figures in the novel (*p. 14*). How were black people treated in *Tom Sawyer*? Were they figures of fun or real people? (This is, intentionally, not an easy question to answer. Students might begin to reflect on how much Jim's language is caricature and how much attitudes to him are fixed and prejudiced.) Slavery is closely related to the 'nigger' question. Note that the word 'nigger' has long been very much out of favour, as it is considered to be disparaging and racist. This whole area can be opened up for discussion as the reading progresses.

It will probably be useful to recall the transcription exercise carried out at the beginning of *Tom Sawyer* and to repeat it, perhaps more briefly, in exactly the same way: taking Jim's first words (*p. 14*) and putting them into more standard English. ('Who dah?' is Who's that? and should not present difficulties.) Readers who have coped with the dialect in *Tom Sawyer* and are used to the idea of *sounding* unusual snatches of dialogue will not find too many problems here. Twain's technique was to transcribe the sounds of speech so the most natural way to cope with these sounds in reading is to try to transcribe them back into a more readily understandable form.

### Language games

Huck's own linguistic peculiarities begin in the first line, so it will be worth stressing that his English is at least two removes from the language students are learning! Students should be encouraged to enjoy this kind of wordplay. If they can make a game of it, it is actually a considerable help in their own grammar learning. Many students enjoy speaking 'imitation Huck' language. As long as a clear idea is maintained of where the deviance lies and how it works this is to be encouraged.

Examples from the first pages include: 'without you have read' (if you haven't read or without having read); 'I never seen anybody but lied' (I never saw (knew) *or* I have never seen (known) anybody who didn't lie'; 'sivilize' (civilize) a key word throughout; 'no longer' (any longer) and so on. The reference to 'grumble a little over the victuals' might have to be explained: it is saying grace, or giving thanks before eating.

### Atmosphere and intention

The first chapter, with Huck's premonitions, gives a foretaste of the atmosphere that will prevail in the novel. Where the first chapter of *Tom Sawyer* was openly comic, here there is no laughter. There is the same insistence on character, and the way the widow wants to bring Huck up echoes some aspects of Tom's relationship with his Aunt Polly. But Huck has never had Tom's degree of simple mischievousness, so there is a more serious, concerned feeling here right from the start.

Each chapter has headings which usefully summarize the content. These should be used for the prediction of what students think will happen in the chapter. They should also pick out which of these headings might be ironic ('Civilizing Huck', for example, in chapter 1).

This will prepare students for the more serious concerns of the novel without losing sight of Twain's constant irony and humour.

### Compare and contrast

If students have kept a reading diary for *Tom Sawyer* it should be to hand all through the reading of *Huckleberry Finn*. In this way quite a few dialect and language queries can be resolved, and many points noted can be expanded upon.

Chapter-by-chapter comparison of the two novels is only really of any help for the first three or four chapters, but it will be very useful in starting off the reading.

Some useful contrasts can be suggested immediately for students to keep as headings while reading the book: first person narration as against third person narration; Huck as central character instead of Tom (is Tom less important in this book than Huck was in *Tom Sawyer*?); how do other characters change and develop, especially Jim?; which characters appear in both novels?; are their roles similar in both?

During reading, students should be encouraged to comment on and weigh up these contrasts as a first step towards evaluating the different intentions and scope of the two books.

There is the same kind of 'down-the-river' running away in both books, but here it is differently motivated, and has much longer-lasting and profound consequences. This introduces the more serious themes and opens up discussion possibilities.

### Summary

As with *Tom Sawyer*, oral summary, while students are reading the book, will be a useful prelude to class discussion. The chapter headings give a useful starting-point for summaries, and can be exploited further than just giving bare facts: What does this heading mean? Is it ironic? Does it tie in with anything that has gone before?

It will also be useful to refer to the headings in discussion on Twain's attitude (ironic, flippant or serious, for instance) to what Huck is narrating, Huck's own attitudes and the readers' reactions. How often can the authorial presence be noticed, and how often is Huck 'pure' Huck? There are no right or wrong answers to this kind of question, obviously, but it will be worth going into this from time to time to judge the book more objectively.

### Character and circumstance

For the first sixteen chapters the novel is principally about Huck and Jim. Their relationship on the river is perhaps the most positive aspect of the whole book. They reach a kind of equality and interdependence which rises above racial stereotypes and the conditioning of Huck's upbringing. The climax of this relationship is in the fog scene at the end of chapter 15, where Huck plays the 'dream' trick on Jim, and has to 'humble myself to a nigger' (*p. 90*).

Encourage students to watch for the times when Huck calls Jim by his name and when he calls him a 'nigger', for it is here that the major ambiguity of Huck's character and of Huck and Jim's relationship lies. Huck never actually escapes from the conditioning of his upbringing in the way he considers 'niggers', despite his relationship with Jim on the raft. When, in chapter 16, they are approaching Cairo, there is for Jim some hope of freedom: to go up the Ohio river to Illinois would be to head for freedom, whereas to continue down the Mississippi would be to go further towards the part of America where slaves were treated worst. The expression 'to be sold down the river' has exactly this implication – of betrayal – and Huck has the constant problem of wrestling with his conscience as to whether or not he can bring himself to betray Jim in this way.

The central passage in this context is in chapter 30 (*p. 206 (final paragraph) to p. 208*) when he tears up the letter. It might be useful to anticipate this passage when students reach the end of chapter 16, as the whole tone of the story changes at that point. How does this scene fit with the relationship between Jim and Huck as students have found it until the end of chapter 16? How do they think the relationship will develop now that there is the possibility of freedom for Jim?

The arrival of the Duke and the King in chapter 19 marks a new stage in the novel. These are classic confidence tricksters, liars and cheats. In a way they are used to represent the corruption of the Shore as opposed to the ideal simplicity of the river (and Huck and Jim's raft). Students will easily be able to pick out their lies right from the beginning, when they claim to be the Duke of Bridgewater (which is then rendered as Bilgewater) and the King of France (*pp. 124–5*). That Huck can be taken in by them is a confirmation of something basically innocent and good in him, perhaps even naïve. Students will find this aspect of his character worth evaluating, and prediction can become a regular feature of the reading as they follow the tricksters through the next few chapters. What do students think (or hope) will become of them?

In a not dissimilar way Phelps's farm (*introduced on p. 212*) can be seen to represent something that is wrong with the society Twain is describing. As in the interlude of the Shepherson–Grangerford feud in chapters 17 and 18 (*pp. 98–118*), when the characters are away from the river they find themselves in a society that is corrupt, incomprehensible, almost meaningless. But at Phelps's farm there is a major difference – Tom Sawyer begins to play a main part in the story. (It is interesting that Huck is actually mistaken for Tom at one point and then becomes rather less important than Tom for some time.)

After the punishment by tarring and feathering of the Duke and the King (at the end of chapter 33 (*p. 224*)) the tone returns to comedy, just when it could easily have moved towards tragedy. Critics sometimes consider this a weakness in the novel. Students might like to discuss what would have happened had Tom not intervened – if Jim had had to go right down the river to the New Orleans area.

The ending, when Huck decides to 'light out for the Territory' (*p. 281*), seeking a newer New World, is sometimes seen as an escape. Is the society Huck runs away from always necessarily corrupt? Is he irresponsible in his reactions to it? Is Tom thoughtless in not revealing Jim's freedom until he does? These are all the kind of open questions the book leaves the reader with, and can be the subject of wide-ranging discussion.

## Black and white

Racial prejudice between blacks and whites is fundamental to the whole book and is used to reflect various kinds of hypocrisy, self-deceit and corruption.

The novel is set before the American Civil War and the term 'abolitionist' occurs frequently. The northern states wanted to abolish slavery and the southern states resisted. So there is a clear political context to the writing. And the problem remains today, with the existence of such groups as the John Birch Society and the Ku Klux Klan. Research projects on these manifestations of continuing prejudice could be organized after the reading, linking the present-day problem to what Huck and Jim lived through in the novel.

But clearly no issue in the novel is 'black and white' in reductively simple terms. So students should be encouraged to pick out and note in their reading diaries some of the polarities that continually emerge. Some of these might be:

POSITIVE
civilization   racial harmony   true   reality   River   nature
north   freedom   companionship   integrity   love

NEGATIVE
Huck's attitudes   attitudes to 'niggers'   false   pretence   Shore
society   south   slavery   solitude   dishonesty   hate

Violence, cruelty, cowardice, unthinking actions and corruption weigh the balance heavily towards the negative. Does this make the novel as a whole negative and pessimistic?

The comic treatment of morally dubious characters is also relevant here. The splendid comic set-pieces in chapter 21 (Shakespeare) and chapter 22 (the circus) with their corruption of language, suspension of disbelief, and the actual enjoyment of falsity, show that we cannot, again, describe the issues in simple 'black-and-white' terms: the reader enjoys the King and the Duke's tricks, shares Huck's willing suspension of disbelief when the drunk comes out of the crowd to ride a circus horse. There is a careful balance between knowingness and innocence here, which necessarily involves the reader in making moral judgements on the characters and their actions, motivations and prejudices.

The question also has to be faced as to how much Jim's own background, upbringing and conditioning have made him what he is. Are black people just as conditioned as whites? How do they see white people? Are whites all the same to blacks, just as blacks may look the same to whites, and have no real individual identity? (An excellent example of this, is after the boat accident (*p. 215*): 'Good gracious! anybody hurt?' 'No'm. Killed a nigger.' 'Well, it's lucky . . .') Have students note as many examples of prejudice-talk they can find, from all sides.

Most of the class discussion will revolve round these themes, but other ideas should not be overlooked: how Huck's point of view influences all we see; how family and environment condition us; America and its life-style; how much pretence there is in all our lives; what friendship and companionship really are. Thematically the novel is a treasure trove.

## Conclusions and evaluation

The kind of conclusions students will draw after reading *Huckleberry Finn* will be very different from those they had after reading *Tom Sawyer*. How much do they see it as a comic novel? How different do they find it from the earlier novel?

Comparison may usefully be made with literature from students' own culture. How much is *Huckleberry Finn* 'a sentimental education'? How much is it a social novel? How much does it reflect present-day American culture and life-styles? Is it peculiarly American, with consequently less relevance to other cultures?

Final conclusions, preferably written, should consider the novel's moral standpoints, its lack of overt judgement, its avoidance of tragedy and the humanity of the characters. Is it optimistic or pessimistic on the whole? Would students recommend it to others?

*Notes prepared by John McRae*